Contents

Cover: The frivolous 'New Woman',
liberated from strait-laced corsets and
decorum. From the German fashion
magazine *Elegante Welt* (1913).
Front endpaper: A futuristic view (1896) of
'The Feminist Battalion at the Barricades'.
Rear endpaper: 'The day after tomorrow'
(1927): emancipated globetrotters in
bathing costumes, beside the new symbols
of freedom

Copyright © 1971: Trevor Lloyd
First published in 1971 by
Macdonald Unit 75
St Giles House 49 Poland St London W1
in the British Commonwealth and
American Heritage Press
551 Fifth Avenue New York NY 10017
in the United States of America
Library of Congress Card Catalogue
Number: 77-957 19
Made and printed in Great Britain by
Purnell and Sons Ltd Paulton Somerset

SUFFRAGETTES INTERNATIONAL

The world-wide campaign for women's rights

Trevor Lloyd

American Heritage Press
General Editor : John Roberts

Chapter 1
Beginnings

In England 'votes for women' meant suffragettes breaking glass and chaining themselves to railings. Events in England were only one part of a movement that was active all over the world, but although their approach was not typical of the long struggle, for a few years they held the centre of the stage.

Perhaps English women were more determined than any of the others, or English men resisted more unreasonably, or perhaps English society was so restrained and restricted that people welcomed the chance to let fly in a cause that they could take seriously. In any case, the militant suffragettes taught political agitators a good many lessons for the future – some of which are being put into practice at the present day.

Most of the women who wanted the vote were entirely conventional, except on this one issue. They were brought up as good strong-minded Victorian pillars of society in an age when Victorianism was not confined to England. Queen Victoria herself disapproved of women who wanted the vote and thought they deserved to be whipped, but in their determination and high-mindedness most of the women who wanted the vote had a lot in common with the Queen of England. Of course, if the Queen herself had been in favour of the vote, it might have made a considerable difference. She could never have announced her opinions publicly, but if people at the top of British society had been reminded of the rights of women by a woman whom they had to take seriously, the story might have been different, and much shorter.

Queen Victoria, and those who admired her, accepted a set of rules and conventions that severely limited the role of women in society and eventually provoked the feminist movement. Some of these conventions look more restricting than they were in fact: for instance, there were very strict rules about what could be written, especially in English-speaking countries. Victorian literature has a heavy air of sexual propriety about it and people today are surprised to find that the private lives of

Left: An early lampoon (1819) on women's fight for equality

8 / 7 / 1

the Victorians were much less restrained than their literature.

The convention that wives should be obedient to their husbands was obeyed some of the time: the husband was expected to be the head of the household, and often lived up to his role. But when the wife was the stronger personality, authority naturally drifted into her hands. This did not help women in the struggle for equality: it encouraged the anti-feminists to say that a skilful and intelligent woman could get her own way by exerting influence on men without any need to possess any legal rights.

But the convention that handicapped women most severely was the idea that a woman's place was in the home. This applied fairly exclusively to women of the upper and middle classes—poor people might have liked women to stay at home, but they could not afford it, except in the sense that a great many working-class women lived in other people's homes as servants.

Women had no place in the professions, except in the Catholic Church, where they were able to join religious orders. They could not become priests or clergymen, which excluded them from a much wider range of positions than it would at the present time. They could not become lawyers or doctors, and they had great difficulty in becoming merchants or traders because of legal restrictions on women's right to inherit or to own property.

'A woman's place is in the home' was a conservative slogan, which described the existing state of affairs and declared that it ought to continue. The right to vote was only one of a number of changes sought in the position of women. When the struggle began, around the middle of the 19th century, women claimed that they needed the vote in order to achieve the other changes. But by the time they got the vote most of the other changes for which they had been asking had already been made: women could go to universities, they could become doctors, they could get divorces if their marriages had collapsed catastrophically, and they could earn their own living.

18th-century beginnings

The upheaval in ideas which accompanied the French Revolution led to some questioning of women's position in society. Jean-Jacques Rousseau, the 18th-century French philosopher, wrote that man was born free, but he showed in his writing (and in the way he treated his wife) **10** ▷

*Far right: The submissive sex—woman as drudge **(top)** and plaything **(bottom)**. **Right:** Women's clubs fulminated against the suffocating female role. **Next page:** 'The salon in the Rue des Moulins', Toulouse-Lautrec's vision of a Paris brothel*

that this was not meant to apply to women. But discussion about the rights of men led on logically to Mary Wollstonecraft's *Vindication of the Rights of Women* in 1792. It did not have much effect, and Horace Walpole called her 'a hyena in petticoats' for her pains, but it was a beginning.

Mary Wollstonecraft paid little attention to the right to vote and did not consider it very important. Few men had the right to vote in 18th-century England, and women were not always without political influence: in the famous 1784 election in Westminster the Duchess of Devonshire had canvassed for Charles James Fox, and had kissed some electors to win their votes. It was not the same as having votes of their own, but women showed no signs of wanting to vote.

In France, Mme Roland played a more serious role in politics during the Revolution. Her salon became the intellectual centre of the Girondin party and she was generally believed to guide her husband's policy while he was Minister of the Interior. It did her no good: she was guillotined by the Jacobins and is now remembered mainly for her comment: 'Liberty, what crimes are committed in your name!' But Mme Roland was obliged to work indirectly: women did not get the vote during the Revolution. Olympe de Gouges petitioned the Constituent Assembly and the Convention for women's rights. The revolutionaries took her seriously and—perhaps because they reckoned that women would oppose the anticlerical aspects of the Revolution—guillotined her too.

In the twenty years between the end of the bloodthirsty period of the French Revolution and the fall of Napoleon in 1815, the most conspicuous political woman in Europe was Mme de Staël. It was not always easy to take her seriously; her love-affairs were conducted at the top of her voice and, although the times were such that few people found them shocking, a great many found them ridiculous. All the same, her constant pressure for freedom of speech and freedom of the press upset Napoleon so much that he hounded her mercilessly. In return she intrigued against him incessantly and her persistence was acknowledged (though of course exaggerated) in the remark that there were three great powers against Napoleon: England, Russia, and Mme de Staël.

This was not a matter of boudoir intrigue; her love-affairs seldom had much to do with her political activity. She conducted a salon which, while not avowedly anti-Napoleon, definitely favoured free speech. She wrote novels, political theory, and literary criticism that attempted to combine the qualities of 18th-century reasonableness with the enthusiasm of the new romantics. For all her political zeal, however, she seems to have

shown no interest in votes for women. Freedom of speech rather than freedom to vote was always her main concern.

The question remained dormant. William Thompson's *Appeal of One Half the Human Race against the Pretensions of the Other Half,* which came out in 1825, was perhaps the first full-fledged statement of the case for giving women the vote but it attracted very little attention. Neither men nor women in England in the first half of the 19th century had any political cause which made women want to take part in politics.

American suffragettes

Things were different in the United States. Abolition of slavery attracted women, who were eager to play an active part in the campaign. Emancipation for women and emancipation for slaves seemed to have something in common: Oberlin College, for instance, was the first college to take women, and it also took Negro students. But at times the presence of women divided the abolitionists; when women were chosen as delegates from the United States to an anti-slavery conference in London, they were not admitted and were sent upstairs to the gallery instead. William Lloyd Garrison, one of the great abolitionist leaders, arrived a little later and insisted on joining the women in the gallery as a protest. But while determined abolitionists like Garrison were ready for women to be active in the movement, the more sedate reformers continued to feel that women should not be seen too much and should not be heard at all.

Reform movements such as the anti-slavery movement were made up of the sort of middle-class people who would have found the Duchess of Devonshire's electoral activity particularly shocking—Jane Austen, who kept her novel-writing a secret from her relations, was much closer to their ideal of what a lady should be. And yet ladies did do a good deal of the more boring work for reform organisations—like raising funds by holding bazaars.

During the 1840s American women grew more and more dissatisfied with the way the various reform organisations treated them. After a temperance organisation had spent almost the whole of a three-day conference arguing whether they should let a woman member give a speech or not, a women's rights meeting was held in July 1848 at Seneca Falls in New York State. Even at

*Top: Mme de Staël **(left)** and Mme de Pompadour, Louis XV's mistress **(right)**: European powers in their own right, who combined strong minds with ease of access to influential bedrooms. **Middle:** An 18th-century French salon, centre of female power. **Bottom:** Early cartoon (1819) of female reformers*

11

this meeting women's right to vote was asserted less confidently than the right to own property, to obtain a divorce, and to enter the professions.

One inhabitant of Seneca Falls was determined to take practical steps to increase women's freedom. Shortly after the meeting Amelia Jenks Bloomer launched a new costume – a calf-length dress over ankle-length pantaloons – which made it distinctly easier for women to walk about and do their work. But the new fashion was regarded as ridiculous and indecent, and during the 1850s women took to ever-wider and less convenient styles of crinolines. Another American, Dr Mary Walker, tried to lead a movement for more practical clothes in the 1860s but nothing came of it. In England Lady Harberton launched the Rational Dress Association in 1880. This was a little more successful because of the spreading enthusiasm for tennis and cycling in the next couple of decades, but on the whole 19th-century women remained determined to dress in a way that severely limited their freedom.

American women went on working for the abolition of slavery, for temperance, and for other good causes, but they became more and more convinced that the causes they supported would advance more quickly if they had the vote. In the 1860s the Civil War raised high hopes. As in all subsequent wars, women took on some of the work of men while the fighting was going on. They showed that they could make use of the opportunity, and they hoped that men would be grateful after the war.

Wyoming presages the future

But when the war was over the politicians of the victorious North decided to introduce complete emancipation for Negroes, including the vote. Women had to wait even though President Johnson would have preferred votes for women to come first. At first they thought it would be a matter of one or two sessions of Congress, but gradually they realised that men's reforming zeal could die down quite quickly in the face of opposition. In the far west something was gained: when the Territory of Wyoming was created in 1869, women were given the vote on a basis of equality, and the inhabitants stuck to their decision despite attempts to push them into abandoning their eccentric ideals.

Men did not mind so much if women were allowed to vote in local elections – they had been given the right to vote in municipal elections in Sweden in 1862 – but voting for the central government was another matter. In any case, Wyoming was not a state – it was only a municipal council ruling several million empty miles.

'Mrs Satan' for President

After the Civil War the fervour of reform in the United States burnt fairly low for some years to come, but a women's suffrage movement had been established in 1869 and it kept the fight alive. It very soon split, as such movements will do, into an activist and a respectable section. The bone of contention was a Mrs Woodhull; she advocated free love and clearly practised it, she ran a stockbroker's office (helped by the friendship of the railroad magnate 'Commodore' Vanderbilt) at a time when Wall Street was much rougher than it is now, and she managed through her connections in Congress to present the women's case to a congressional committee at Washington for the first time.

She was an ideal leader if women were to get the vote in a single determined rush, but a liability if it came down to a long slow round of lobbying and arguing and proving that women would not do anything rash or unconventional if they had the vote. The activists in the National Woman Suffrage Association naturally supported Victoria Woodhull, and the respectable American Woman Suffrage Association equally naturally disapproved of her. It was a struggle between New York, her home base, where her behaviour was not completely unacceptable, and the other areas where the Suffrage Associations were strong, which tended to agree when she was nicknamed Mrs Satan. Victoria Woodhull ran for President in 1872 (there was nothing to stop her being a candidate), took up spiritualism, and died fifty years later as the wife of an English banker—her sister Tennessee, who had supported her in all her activities, did even better, and died Lady Cook. Victoria Woodhull's career left the American suffrage societies divided for twenty years, though probably no organisation could have made progress during the Gilded Age and the loss of interest in reform that followed the Civil War and Reconstruction.

Women's suffrage became an issue, though with much less preparation, in Great Britain in the 1860s. The philosopher John Stuart Mill had been elected to Parliament in 1865, and when the second Reform Bill was being debated in 1867 he moved an amendment to give votes to women. It was defeated, 194 to 73, but the minority was large enough to surprise and encourage its supporters. For the rest of the century backbenchers moved Private Members' Bills in most sessions of Parliament; this was good publicity for votes for women, but no government took any interest in the suggestion, so opponents of the change could always stop it by talking the Bills out and never letting them come to a vote.

Left: An idealistic French allegory of universal suffrage, 1848

13

Mill was defeated in the 1868 general election, and the next year he published his book *On the Subjection of Women*. He pointed out a great many ways in which women's legal position was inferior to that of men, and argued that the best way to change this was to give women the vote. In fact, the position of women was already changing without the help of the vote. Mill pointed out that married women were not allowed by the law to have any property of their own—extravagant husbands could spend all their own money and could then go on to waste their wives' money as well. But in a matter of a dozen years this abuse had been put right, and wives could keep their own money, while the question of votes passed more or less out of sight.

In France Léon Richier published his book *The Rights of Women* in 1869. The next year, when the Second Empire fell and was replaced by a republic, the prospects for women might appear to have improved under a constitution which was based on universal suffrage. Mme Barbarousse claimed the right to vote on the grounds that *tout français* had been enfranchised; in 1885 the courts declared that, at least so far as the franchise went, 'Frenchmen' did not embrace 'French women'. But here again the tendency to change, unaffected by the vote, could be seen. The *Code Napoléon,* produced at the beginning of the century, had laid down strict rules that placed women in an inferior position: it was accepted as law in France throughout the changes of constitution during the 19th century, and it had a considerable effect in defining the position of women to their disadvantage in a number of other countries as well. Yet it was in the 1880s, when women were being told that the law could not be interpreted in a way that gave them the vote, that the attitude of the *Code Napoléon* was relaxed and divorce was permitted under certain circumstances.

The main reason for the improvement in women's position, in France and elsewhere, was that women could get better jobs than before. Country women had always worked in the fields before they married—after marriage they went on working in the fields, and they withered under the strain of fieldwork combined with running the house. If they did not get married, they could make a little money spinning—hence the word 'spinsters'. Industrialisation and the move to the towns opened up a great many new jobs for men, but not so many for women at first. Spinning and weaving were still the women's jobs; the lucky ones got jobs in the hot, damp

Right: Jules Girardet's painting of the arrest in 1883 of Louise Michel, the celebrated French anarchist who played a leading part in the struggle for improved conditions for the poor

cotton factories, and the less fortunate had to work at home, trying to accept a low enough wage to compete with machinery. Thomas Hood's *The Song of the Shirt*, about an underpaid seamstress, did not stray from the facts, as the British House of Commons found when it investigated conditions in the 'sweated' trades – sewing or making matchboxes or stitching clothes together in the early years of this century.

The 'life of shame'

Trapped in this position of few jobs and low wages, women inevitably took to prostitution. According to middle-class legend, any woman who took to the streets was branded for ever. This was by no means always the case; obviously it was a dangerous job, with rough clients and a much larger chance of venereal disease than at the present day, but all the evidence suggests that there was an astonishingly large number of prostitutes in large cities and that they very often married and settled down when their working days were over.

In the 1890s Bernard Shaw's play *Mrs Warren's Profession* caused a great deal of fuss by suggesting that a girl from the working class was much better off as a prostitute than at work in a white-lead factory where she was likely to die a slow and painful death from phosphorus poisoning. The play was banned in London by the Lord Chamberlain, though in New York the examining magistrate said that it was fit to perform.

The play also had a message of hope because Mrs Warren's daughter could hope for a respectable and more permanent job as an actuary. This was rather an optimistic ending; the young heroine of the play had just come top of the mathematics examination at Cambridge University (a topical point, for Phillippa Fawcett, daughter of the great suffragist leader Millicent Fawcett, managed this in 1890), and so she was eminently employable. Her position, with such rare qualifications, was as unusual as those of the girls at the top of her mother's profession who rose to international celebrity, like Cora Pearl, a leading figure in the demi-monde of Napoleon III, or Mrs Langtry, who was the friend of respectable men like Gladstone although it was quite clear that she was being financially supported by her lover, the Prince of Wales (later Edward VII).

An ordinary middle-class girl would not be able to start work as an actuary, just as she would have been very ill-advised to imagine that she could preserve her social standing as well as Mrs Langtry, if she plunged into

Left: 19th-century male attitudes to woman: the slave of her domineering husband (top), and the tender innocent (bottom)

what respectable Victorians would call a 'life of shame'. The question still remained: how could the middle-class girl earn a living? A few very brilliant women supported themselves as authors and journalists: Harriet Martineau's success as a journalist in England in the mid-19th century showed that it could be done. But when a great writer like Charlotte Brontë had to support herself, with some difficulty, as a teacher, the prospects for women were not good.

'Nightingale nurses'

Florence Nightingale won a unique position during the Crimean War; she organised hospitals and saved the British army from the worst results of its bad organisation and failure to make provision for the cruel winter of 1854-55. And for the next forty years she used the great prestige gained in the Crimea as an adviser on matters of government medical policy. She made nursing into a respectable profession that women could join without being taken for the drunken Mrs Gamp of Dickens's novel. She also made it scientific. At a time when doctors had very few drugs and anaesthetics, nursing was even more important for the patient's survival than at the present day. 'Nightingale nurses', instructed according to her principles, steadily raised hospital standards in England and in other countries.

These nurses were still not well-paid, partly because people thought of nursing as a way of life for devoted women with private means like Florence Nightingale herself, and partly because of the situation on the continent of Europe, where orders of nuns like the *soeurs de charité* worked as nurses under vows of poverty. In the middle of the 19th century they had been providing much more conscientious service than was available in most Protestant countries.

But in spite of Florence Nightingale's efforts to raise nursing standards, by the end of the century the nursing orders had heavily diluted their numbers with lay helpers who were not much better than the pre-Nightingale nurses had been. Reform was inevitable. At the beginning of the 20th century, Anna Hamilton published a thesis on nursing that encouraged the doctors in France to take action: they set up schools of nursing first at Bordeaux and then in several other cities including Paris. Municipal councils co-operated, partly out of a desire for better nursing and partly as a move in the campaign against the religious orders in the aftermath of the Dreyfus Case. The nursing orders were driven out of

Marché
Bêtes à Corn

Right: 'Women for sale'—a French view of the Englishman's market-place attitude to marriage in the early 19th century

their positions. Similar developments took place in Belgium: after a quarrel with a nursing order, the anticlerical Dr Depage decided to launch a training scheme for nurses along Nightingale lines. An English nurse was needed to be the first director, and in 1907 the job was given to Edith Cavell.

But these changes did not much alter the economic situation. When Ibsen wrote *The Doll's House* in 1873, the play ended with Nora, a middle-class housewife, walking out of her husband's house and slamming the door. A great lady who ran a large household was doing a full-time administrative job, and a working-class housewife looking after home and family had more than enough to do. But in middle-class homes it was expected that the work would be done by servants, and the housewife had no purpose in life except to be admired and played with by her husband. But when Nora slammed the door, what was she to do next? Earning a living was probably even harder for a respectable woman on the continent of Europe than in England: George Sand (who often wore men's clothes as well as taking a man's name) gained fame through her novels and notoriety by her affair with Chopin; in the 1860s Rosa Bonheur won some position as a painter; and a little later Sarah Bernhardt attained universal renown as an actress. But women like these were exceptional and nobody would call them respectable or consider them any encouragement for giving women the vote.

The seed-bed of the suffragist movement was the increase in the number of respectable middle-class jobs open to women in the second half of the 19th century. In the United States, Elizabeth Blackwell was able to open up the way to becoming a doctor and later played a considerable role in medical organisation during the Civil War. But in England in the 1850s there was bitter resistance to pioneer women like Elizabeth Garrett Anderson and Sophia Jex-Blake. Hospitals and colleges for medical education changed their rules of admission for the specific purpose of keeping women out and, when the legal barriers had been overcome, the medical students tried to exclude the women by jostling and insulting and pelting them. The behaviour of the Edinburgh students was just like that of white people in the American South anxious to prevent integration of their schools a hundred years later, and it was strongly suspected that the professors encouraged this display of student disorder. But admission to the medical profession was not always a sign of how public opinion would react to votes for

Top right: A French satire on women in the civil service (1869). Bottom right: Women type-setters. Right: Seamstresses

women: in 1870 — by which time there were already 575 women doctors in the United States — both France and Sweden allowed women to become doctors, though public opinion was much less tolerant of women's emancipation in France than in Sweden.

Women had been employed as teachers for many years, and the expansion of education (combined with the reduction in the size of classes) in the 19th century increased the number of jobs. But a high standard of respectability was always expected of school-teachers: school boards preferred to employ unmarried women only, and even in the most Protestant of countries women teachers were expected to behave like members of a strict religious order. Teachers were expected to behave as though they had taken vows of chastity, obedience, and poverty — as was shown by the teacher training college in the 1880s which refused to install baths on the grounds that it would not be a good idea to give teachers a taste for luxury which they would never again be able to afford. School-teachers were an advance-guard of women who could earn their own living, but they were not able to do much to strengthen the suffragettes.

The typist revolution

The decisive shift in the economic position of women came with the expansion and simplification of office work. In the middle of the 19th century the office clerk possessed qualities which were in short supply — literacy and honesty with money. By the end of the century these qualities, though still necessary, were no longer in short supply. There seemed to be an endless stream of young girls prepared to be book-keepers or 'typewriters', the late 19th-century word for typists. Of course many of these girls could now earn their living if the need arose; they did not have to concentrate on finding a husband, and if they failed to do so they did not have to look forward to becoming pitied dependants of their families.

As the years have gone by, this stream of girls going into office work has broadened into a flood. Today office work has replaced domestic service as the dominant occupation among women in Europe and North America. But this change had not taken place by the time of the great struggle for the vote: domestic servants were still relatively easy to find, and young ladies who worked in offices — usually middle-class pioneers — were still a novelty, though a novelty which was rapidly becoming a necessity. For some decades the telephone system was worked manually by girls who plugged lines into sockets to put calls through; if telephone calls were still to be put through in this way today, the whole female population of the United States would be at work putting plugs

into sockets. But the telephone girl was in her time one sign that women were gaining greater economic freedom.

Ladies complaining about the servant problem would say that the young girls had gone off to work in factories. This does not seem very likely. Girls who were servants in the better sort of family (these complaints about the shortage of servants always came from ladies who explained how attractive their homes were) went into the simpler type of office work rather than into factories. But the servant problem had not really reached a crisis before 1914, and the girl in the office was still the middle-class pioneer rather than the ordinary girl who takes it for granted that she can dive into the typing pool even if she cannot become anything more interesting.

At the same time as office jobs became easier to find, and servants became harder to keep, housekeeping became simpler. Shopping had been in the past an immensely time-consuming business in which customers went out and bargained with shopkeepers about each item on sale. The Quakers in England and America are said to have been among the first shopkeepers to stop bargaining and put a price-ticket on their goods below which they refused to go.

The Quakers' fixed price was not only more truthful but it was also more convenient for shoppers, who could get what they wanted quickly. Bargaining went on, even in prosperous countries, among the very poor and the very rich, buying in small quantities or buying very special products. But for most things bargaining became difficult with the growth of large manufacturing or food-processing chains. When sugar was put into neatly-wrapped packets—by the Tate family (the Lyle family was in golden syrup)—something closer to a standard price per packet was charged than in the days when the grocer scooped it out of a barrel and weighed it himself. And the packaged food was less likely to be adulterated; the local grocer had a nasty habit of putting a little sand into his sugar barrel, but the large food processors were more careful of their reputations. Food in tin-cans had appeared by the end of the 19th century and made life easier, though it was soon regarded as a sign of bad housekeeping.

Changes in home furnishing also saved time. Victorian furniture was heavy and hard to move, and the fashion for quantities of decorations, ornaments, and knick-knacks involved an immense amount of dusting. And for most of the century the dusting was made all the

*Left: Fashion sheds its weight. **Top:** 'The Bum Shop' by Rowlandson (c. 1780). **Middle:** 'Bloomerism' (c. 1850). **Bottom:** The revelation of the ankle (c. 1914) and the knee (c. 1925)*

grimier because rooms were lit by candles or by a sooty sort of gas-lamp. In the 1880s the gas-mantle reduced the sootiness of this sort of lamp, and electricity provided the first completely clean form of illumination. The general clutter of the Victorian home began to disappear in the face of the attitude expressed in William Morris's slogan 'Have nothing in your home that you do not know to be useful or believe to be beautiful'. As the flood-tide of knick-knacks receded, women acquired more freedom simply because they had more time. Other little inventions helped: chopping up soap bars into soapflakes made washing easier, and so did the early washing-machines which took women away from the washing-tub and the mangle. The vacuum-cleaner came a bit later, but there is a moving passage in Arnold Bennett about the Ewbank floor-sweeper, which at the end of the century was the last word in modernity, at least in the homes of Great Britain's industrial areas.

These changes made it easier for middle-class women to earn their own living because they had more time, and also meant that women who did not have to earn their own living could spend much less time looking after the house. The liberation of young girls from the need to find a husband as soon as possible was one of the foundations of the movement to get the vote; their leaders were married or respectably widowed women with plenty of time for the tasks of organisation. It was said that the suffragettes were women who had failed to find husbands or, as Marie Corelli, a fashionable novelist who was never sorry to find a way to remind people of her charms, put it in 1907, 'One never sees any pretty women among those who clamour for their rights.'

Opponents of giving votes to women said that clever and attractive women could persuade men to see things their way, and thus had political power without needing a vote. Why it was only the attractive women who deserved to have political power was never explained, but the argument was often heard that women who went out to ask for their rights were in some way dissatisfied with home life or their failure to find a husband and set up a home. The leaders of the movement must, in fact, have had remarkably happy homes: without the loyal support of their families they could never have got their work accomplished.

Left: Revolution in the home: 1874 'washing, wringing, and mangling machine' **(top left)**; *1873 cooker* **(top right)**; *1909 vacuum cleaner* **(bottom left)**; *sewing machine* **(bottom right)**

Chapter 2
Good Causes

Several political issues not directly concerned with the right to vote were fought in the last decades of the century. Problems like licensed prostitution were in some ways even more difficult than the fight for the vote. In the 1860s the British House of Commons had passed the Contagious Diseases Acts which said that in towns where troops were billeted, women suspected of being prostitutes could be compulsorily examined for venereal disease — and in the days before Wassermann tests examination was an unpleasant process. Compulsory examination upon suspicion inevitably led to trouble when the examiners mistakenly picked on respectable women, but nobody expected the respectable women to do anything about it. But they had in Josephine Butler a remarkably talented leader: they put forward candidates at by-elections, asked questions at general elections and lobbied MPs while Parliament was sitting. This was one of the first pressure-groups run mainly by women to be successful; after about fifteen years of struggle and argument the Acts were repealed.

The compulsory examinations of respectable women provided the campaign with a certain amount of its propaganda, but the deeper criticism of the Acts was that they treated women as though they were just instruments for men's pleasure, who ought to be supervised for the convenience of the men. The Acts had been seen as a considerable interference with liberty in England; in countries like France and Italy, where the trade was already neatly supervised and was run by brothels which were to a greater or lesser extent state-approved, women were being much more systematically treated as instruments of pleasure. Josephine Butler went on from her success with the British House of Commons to help direct European agitation against the system of brothels. This was a much longer task, but when the League of Nations was set up after the First World War its social agencies ac-

Left: *The bicycle was a harbinger and symbol of emancipated woman. Decorative cycling motifs from an Italian magazine*

cepted the need to fight the 'white slave trade' which kid-napped girls and forced them to work as prostitutes by keeping them locked up in brothels. This part of its work met with some success; and after the Second World War licensed and approved brothels were closed down in France and Italy. Prostitution still goes on, but at least it is to a large extent a trade that girls have chosen for themselves and can leave when they want to.

In the United States brothels existed mainly as a con-venient way of rewarding the police for not enforcing laws against prostitution. As such they were not a direct interference with girls' freedom in the same way as French and Italian brothels were and so were less objec-tionable to reformers of Mrs Butler's views.

The Demon Drink
The campaign for the prohibition of alcoholic drink in the United States was on a far larger scale than anything Mrs Butler dreamed of, but at some points it was com-parable. Women played a considerable role in the strug-gle; the Women's Christian Temperance Union was al-ways prominent in local referendums and in elections—it was dry policy to support any party, Republican, Demo-crat, or Populist, which was ready to give convincing dry pledges. And at the level of direct action, Carrie Nation (a woman whose religious zeal had been a little too much for her balance of mind) used to go round with her axe, march into saloons, and chop up the bar and break the glassware, bottles, and all.

The campaign against the Contagious Diseases Acts in England was kept separate from the movement to get the vote, in case it made votes for women seem an unrespec-table cause; in the United States the leaders of the cam-paign for the vote tried not to become associated with the Prohibition agitation, but their prudent efforts were in vain. Prohibition would appeal to women if it appealed to anyone; the pleasures of getting drunk were usually reserved for men (though not always), and their wives then had to cope with a violent husband who had poured too much of the housekeeping money down his throat. The drunkard's wife was in a pitiable situation, and the propaganda of the Prohibitionists lost no opportunity to remind everyone about it. And so female supporters of prohibition quite naturally said that women ought to be given the vote so that they could vote against the 'demon drink'. Women who wanted the vote often co-operated with this approach and claimed that drunkenness was one of the many evils that would be reduced once women had the vote.

But whatever the real relationship between heavy drinking and votes for women, the liquor interests,

brewers, distillers, publicans, and saloon-owners, and the ordinary man who liked a drink all came to believe that 'votes for women' meant Prohibition for men. And as a result any opponent of Prohibition was a potential opponent of votes for women. The supporters of votes for women may have overestimated the importance of the liquor interest, and attributed to its hostility failures that were really due to the fact that a great many men were quite satisfied with things as they were, and did not see why votes for women would be any improvement. All the same, the liquor trade did provide some organisation for the opponents of enfranchisement.

The trapped wife

For whatever reason, the 1870s and 1880s were not a period of progress for women on the issue of the suffrage, though other changes went forward, or at least became established as causes which could expect success. The attack on the existing structure of marriage was beginning. *The Doll's House* had attacked the falsity of a marriage which was, by the standards of the time, peaceful and happy, but many marriages were much less successful, and they were very hard to dissolve. In the United States the rules varied from state to state but tended not to be accommodating; in England adultery by the wife was grounds for divorce but adultery by the husband would serve only if it was accompanied by cruelty; in almost all of Europe divorce was unthinkable though it might be legal. In the upper classes these things could be managed, though at the cost of considerable loss of social standing; in the urban working class there was frequently no marriage ceremony, and so no problem of divorce. In the middle class the indissolubility of marriage was more of a burden, and the reaction against it was sometimes extreme.

In Manchester in the late 1870s the youthful and impetuous Emmeline Goulden put it to Dr Richard Pankhurst that marriage was so unsatisfactory that they should form a 'free union'; Dr Pankhurst was a scrupulous man, and he pointed out to her that the laws and the economic conditions made free love as dangerous as marriage for a woman. They duly got married, and until his death twenty years later they carried on the work of agitation for a great many radical causes without attracting much attention.

The great American dancer, Isadora Duncan, was even

Left: 'Le style c'est la femme'—a French cartoon on fashion.
Left from top: Baby-doll for brothel madame, the instant undress, the artistic, the chic. *Right:* The fetishistic, the homemade replica, the lure of beauty-spots, the small dressmaker

younger when she decided 'I would live to fight against marriage and for the emancipation of women' — according to her autobiography she was twelve years old, and the child of an unhappy marriage. She lived up to her programme, though eventually she decided that the system of marriage accompanied by divorce on demand by either party which had been established in Russia for the first few years after the Revolution was satisfactory. But before this she had shown that what she considered the important aspect of emancipation was the right of a woman to have children without having a husband. This, of course, was an extreme attitude but more moderate versions of the same idea were beginning to be heard fairly widely.

Public opinion was not prepared to accept this, but many people admitted that marriage could be a trap for women which deprived them of their freedom and left them at the mercy of a man whom they might have married without sufficient thought — of course, a marriage might be unsatisfactory for the husband, but in the last resort he could always abandon his home and desert his wife, a drastic solution that was virtually out of the question for her unless she had a job or a private income to fall back on.

Easier divorce and early birth control
In the United States, from about 1890 onwards, states altered their divorce laws in a way that made it easier to end marriages. This was not caused by votes for women; the changes in divorce law usually came before women had been given the right to vote. The increasing influence of women had some effect: women took an active interest in politics, and helped with party organisation, so that men might be concerned to conciliate women in politics even before they got the vote, but this indirect pressure was not likely to be decisive by itself. In fact, the men also wanted easier divorce laws.

Easier divorce did increase women's freedom and so did birth control. A certain amount had been known about birth control techniques for centuries, but the idea that the knowledge might be spread more widely as a way of fighting poverty and freeing women from bondage to child-bearing was a 19th-century development.

People had believed that if the poor had a little more money they would only spend it on having larger families. John Stuart Mill seems to have been among the first to see that this perpetuation of poverty could be avoided if

*Right: The first telephonists. **Top right:** Man's 'dissipation' provokes protest in an Arizona billiard-room. **Bottom right:** Caricature showing how the piano is taught at a girls' school*

the poor learnt something about birth control, which did not help his reputation. (Gladstone withdrew from a committee for a memorial to Mill when he learnt about this aspect of his work.) In the 1870s there were limited campaigns in England to provide advice and information; Charles Bradlaugh and Mrs Annie Besant were tried and convicted for circulating obscene literature, though the judge made it clear that he regarded the verdict as unjustified.

Giving advice and information in the United States was even harder—there was something very like a crusade to stop it. Anthony Comstock, who made a lifelong career out of seeking out all sorts of obscene literature and other manifestations of vice, persuaded state legislatures to pass new laws to prevent the sale of contraceptives and the spread of information, making it very hard for reformers to help the poor who went on having large families, many of whom died very young (in some cases helped on their way by their parents, who could not face the prospect of another mouth to feed).

Bradlaugh and Mrs Besant would have been regarded as disreputable even if they had had nothing to do with birth control; they were atheist lecturers and Bradlaugh was a declared republican—the pair of them stood in an old radical tradition which believed that Church and Crown were the enemies of the people, and that the way to help the people was to tell them what the world was really like.

Mrs Besant moved on from birth control to socialism. By the 1880s she was one of the best orators in England; in 1888 she organised and inspired a strike of the London match girls, and when the newly-founded Fabian Society published its *Fabian Essays in Socialism* in 1889, she was the only contributor who was already well known. If she had remained in English politics she would almost certainly have become a leader in the struggle for votes for women, and would have been a rare example of an unhappily married woman in the movement—she had been married to a clergyman, and had only become prominent after leaving him. But she gave up socialism for theosophy and, apart from a brief moment in the First World War when she helped persuade the Indian Congress Party to take a more militant line in the struggle for independence, she left the political scene for ever.

Her influence may have lingered on in another odd way; in 1907 Bernard Shaw wrote a play, *Getting Married,* **36** ▷

Right: The girl of genteel background was carefully protected from the kind of harsh reality her working-class counterpart —such as this young girl operating complex machinery in a South Carolina cottonmill, c. 1900—was continually exposed to

The New Woman

In the Park

In 1852 Florence Nightingale had inveighed against the system of stifling gentility that oppressed all members of her class and sex: 'Give us back our suffering, suffering rather than indifferentism . . . for out of suffering may come the cure. Better have pain than paralysis.' The new spirit born of the struggle for equality manifested itself in a variety of fashionable or forward-looking freedoms: in the new sport of bicycling, for instance **(bottom right:** 'the Championess'), which baffled so many chaperones; in the scramble for tobacco **(top right)**; and in the founding of women's university colleges **(below:** Bryn Mawr College, USA). When G.K. Chesterton wrote, 'Twenty million young women rose to their feet with the cry, "We will not be dictated to", and proceeded to become stenographers,' he was, as usual, not being wholly fair. Even an office job was an advance on the times when all serious activities were left to the men and woman's role was to be passive and stay-at-home

THE ROAD

OUR RICH AUNT JESSICA FAVOURS THE TIME HONOURED CHURCHWARDEN

THE MATER PREFERS A MEERCHAUM.

OUR SISTERS AND OUR COUSINS SPORT THE DAINTY CIGARETTE

"NOW I'M GRAN'MA"

SARAH JANE LIKES A BRIAR

THE LADIES OF THE EAST HAVE INDULGED IN THE FRAGRANT WEED FOR AGES.

THE GREAT SMOKE QUESTION.

The Ladies (bless 'em) take it up.

in which the characters discuss the disadvantages of marriage, and wonder whether it might not be better for men and women to set up relationships by individually devised contracts. This was a bright idea, but Shaw did not really pursue it consistently, and he let the opponents of contract win the argument too easily. Perhaps the reason was that Shaw had already had to face the issue because in her Fabian days Annie Besant had been closely enough attached to him to suggest that they should enter into a contract (she was, of course, still married). When Shaw heard the terms she proposed he said it would take away even more of his freedom than marriage. He was probably exaggerating – any relationship with a personality as strong as Annie Besant would soon have restricted his freedom just as much.

New opportunities

The 'new woman' of the 1890s, who was just beginning to go to Bernard Shaw's plays, was the recruiting material that the suffrage movement needed. She played the new game of lawn tennis, and she benefited from the decline in fashion of billiards, an all-male game. She bicycled, and had a chance to make unexpected acquaintances – it was relatively easy to chaperone a girl at a dance but hard to provide a chaperone for a lady-cyclist, unless it was another relatively emancipated lady-cyclist.

If she was more serious-minded, it was easier for her to take an interest in social reform. By the end of the century Jane Addams had established Hull House as a centre for social work in Chicago which became a school for training social reformers (among them Mackenzie King, later Prime Minister of Canada for over twenty years). In England Miss Beatrice Potter found no real difficulties in her way when she wanted to find out about the problems of poverty in the East End of London – she disguised herself as a poor woman looking for work making cheap shirts, but it soon became so clear that her talent was for organisation rather than sewing that she was invited to marry the manager's son and settle down to run the business. Despite her excursions into the slums she continued to move in the best society. After she had married Sidney Webb, another early Fabian, they used her social position to get in touch with political leaders whom they then lobbied on behalf of their various crusades for social reform.

Early in her career of social investigation and research Beatrice Potter had been so far from feeling handicapped by her position as a woman that she signed a petition drawn up by Mrs Humphrey Ward the novelist, deploring the agitation for giving women the vote. Later on she decided that this had been a mistake and she became

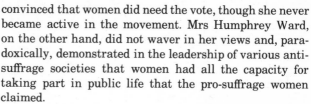

convinced that women did need the vote, though she never became active in the movement. Mrs Humphrey Ward, on the other hand, did not waver in her views and, paradoxically, demonstrated in the leadership of various anti-suffrage societies that women had all the capacity for taking part in public life that the pro-suffrage women claimed.

One interesting index of the changing position of women was provided by the Nobel Prizes set up at the end of the 19th century: Mme Marie Curie shared the prize for Physics in 1903 and in 1911 won the Chemistry prize outright for her work of refining radium out of pitchblende and investigating related problems of radio-activity (only one other person, Linus Pauling, has won two Nobel prizes). In 1905 Baroness von Suttner was awarded the Peace prize, though to some extent this was just a compliment to Alfred Nobel, the dead founder of the prizes, because the Baroness had been his secretary for the last years of his life. In 1909 the Literature prize was awarded to the Swedish poet, Selma Lagerlöf; her writing was rather consciously elevating in tone and she concentrated on the sort of subjects thought suitable for women, such as the beauties of home life. The Literature prize is notoriously awarded, to a much greater extent than any of the others, on the basis of making sure that no important group feels left out, and the award to Selma Lagerlöf may have been intended as a compliment to women in general.

Left: *Women in the headlines: Isadora Duncan* **(top left)**, *the emancipated woman par excellence; Mrs Emmeline Pankhurst* **(top right)**, *protagonist of total war on anti-suffragist and neutral alike, and one of the greatest orators of her time; Marie Curie* **(bottom)**, *Nobel Prize-winner, together with her husband Pierre*

Chapter 3
The Focus on the Suffrage

Although the position of women had changed in so many ways between the middle of the 19th century and the end, the question of votes for women had hardly moved. Between 1870 and 1890 there was no change at all but in the 1890s there were the first hints of a revival of interest. When Wyoming became a state of the Union in 1890, after a struggle with Congress, the women kept their votes. This meant the women would vote for Congressmen and for President. Until then women's votes in Wyoming had been the equivalent of unmarried English women's right to vote in municipal elections if they had the necessary property qualification. In 1893 the reforming Liberal-Labour government in New Zealand gave women the vote, and thus for the first time women had as much electoral power as men. Even this did not really have to be taken seriously: New Zealand was just a faraway scrap of the British Empire, and not a sovereign state.

The anti-suffrage forces drew their real emotional strength from a feeling (accepted as deeply by women as by men) that women were meant to be dependent rather than equal. However, when they had to provide arguments, they very often said that some areas of activity were particularly appropriate for women—they did not say that men should keep out of these areas, but they did assert that women should stick to them. The home, of course, was the real place for women, but it was accepted that in public life perhaps education and municipal affairs were also suitable for women.

This rationalised giving a few women municipal votes and letting them sit on school boards in England, though not on county councils.

The enemies of votes for women found it reassuring that the new idea was flourishing only in out-of-the-way places. In the 1890s three more states in the western USA joined Wyoming, and Western Australia and South Aus-

Top left: Pioneers of women's enfranchisement in the northwestern states of the USA. Equality of the sexes was usual in the wild West. Bottom: American caricature of women voters

39

tralia (two of the smaller states) enfranchised women. It hardly seemed likely that the example of these distant areas, out on the frontiers of civilisation, would be followed by great and established governments like those of Great Britain, Germany, and the United States.

In one important way Australia, New Zealand, and the American West were typical of what the rest of the world was going to become. In Europe, or on the eastern seaboard of the United States, a woman could be a lady: what it mainly required was good manners and enough money to have servants. In the areas where women first got the vote it was notoriously difficult to keep servants. Girls who went out to the wilder parts of the English-speaking world found it so easy to get a husband that they had no need to go and work for someone else; their husbands could earn a living for themselves, but could never earn enough to employ servants. The decline in the number of servants has gone on at about the same rate as the spread of votes for women: the example set on the frontiers of civilisation, not in the drawing-room, has been followed.

Women and democracy

The people who wanted to keep women out of important political questions, and thought they ought to stay at home, usually also distrusted the capacity of other men to handle these problems. Determined opponents of votes for women tended to be more or less explicitly anti-democratic. Reformers said that if the voice of the people could be heard, governments would be nobler in their actions, and giving votes to women would have a particularly purifying effect. The more democratic the organisation, the more likely it was to include votes for women in its programme.

After getting the vote, women were a little more ready to vote for a conservative or right-wing party than men, but in the last years of the 19th century it always looked as though women were on the left in politics. In Russia, where the constitution was described as 'despotism tempered by assassination', the Nihilists were determined that assassination should become more frequent; they killed Tsar Alexander II in 1881, and they were a threat to Tsars and ministers for years to come. Women played a considerable part in their secret organisations and the enemies of the Tsar asserted that the political police always tortured women on a basis of perfect equality with men.

Top right: Belligerent women in New York parade for better working conditions. Bottom right: The House of Representatives politely receives a deputation of female suffragists, early 1871

40

'Red Rosa'

Until 1907 women in Germany were in theory not allowed to belong to political organisations, but this was not strictly enforced. The sternly Marxist Social Democratic Party was committed to the principle of equality, and was ready to practise it. Clara Zetkin rose to a position of importance in the party while it was still banned by Bismarck's legislation, and a little later she was joined by one of the most remarkable of all women who have gone into politics: Rosa Luxemburg ('Red Rosa', as she was nicknamed, to her disgust). Of course, she could not be elected to the Reichstag, but the Social Democrats attached little importance to the Reichstag because it had so little power, and regarded party conferences as the really central political activity. At conferences Rosa was in her element: she was a speaker of great power, a rigid Marxist, and a forceful logician.

Inside the party a few of her opponents tried to arouse feeling against her by pointing out that she was a woman, and Jewish, and Polish, but the Social Democrats were fair-minded and paid very little attention to any of these issues. Rosa herself found time, in the intervals of a great deal of work in Germany, to encourage the Polish and the Russian parties of the left. Votes for women she simply took for granted: obviously any socialist community would give women equality, but the important thing was to establish socialism and not allow reforming energy to be led off into the essentially bourgeois question of votes for women. This may have seemed rather harsh; however, it was what quite a number of men on the left believed as well. They accepted the principle of votes for women, but they were always afraid that it was going to be used to hold up other reforms.

The French parties of the left shared this worry about votes for women. By the beginning of the century a few Frenchwomen were beginning to stage demonstrations for the right to vote, and French reforming politicians all admitted that they had a good case. The Socialist Viviani raised the issue in the Chamber of Deputies for the first time in 1901.

The French Union for Women's Suffrage was launched under the leadership of Mme Braunsching, in 1909, but it did not make much progress. The Radicals were convinced that women would vote as their priests told them — too many freethinking Radicals had devout wives for them to trust women with the vote. The result of their conviction that votes for women would reinforce the parties of the right was that French women had to wait till after the Second World War to get the vote. And their assessment of the situation was not unjustified. When women did get the vote they supported the *Mouvement*

Républicain Populaire (MRP), which was the most consciously Roman Catholic Party. It was also the party most devoted to social reform without drastic changes in society, and this is the sort of political attitude that women seem to prefer—they are perhaps readier than men to respond to abuses and cases of injustice, but they feel that a radical change in society opens up the risk of disturbance and violence.

Change and the old order

In fact, the Church itself was rather hostile to the demand for votes for women, and felt that this would make them more independent and would break up the family. But more important than the hostility of the Church was the fact that in general the Roman Catholic countries had not become as urbanised and industrialised as the Protestant countries. As a result, at the beginning of the 20th century women were in a weaker position to ask for their rights in Catholic countries. And, it is probably also true to say, they were much less interested in asking for them.

So, by 1900, women had a good chance of getting the vote in urbanised, industrialised countries, where they could get office jobs and where servants were becoming difficult to find; in other countries the problem was not much discussed. But there was one other factor to consider, and it probably explains why votes for women caused so much trouble and disturbance in England.

In a new country, or in an old country when it undergoes great upheaval, change is relatively easy. Wyoming could give its women votes: it was giving its whole population votes for the first time. The other American states which gave women the vote in the 1890s were only just emerging from being territories and becoming states. By the beginning of the 20th century women's suffrage was accepted as the modern thing to believe in; every new country wants to be modern; and so every new country was sympathetic to votes for women. And an unexpectedly large number of new countries emerged in the 20th century. It was in older, established countries that changes were harder.

Left: *A parade of hats at a suffrage meeting in Paris, 1908*

43

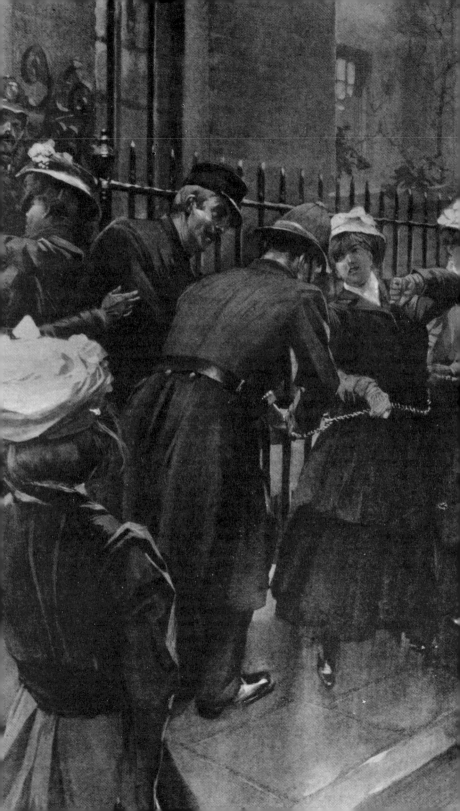

Chapter 4
Two Ways: England and Scandinavia

In England changes did take place, but they happened quietly and people tried to ignore them. But the question of votes for women — in fact, the whole question of women — was hard to ignore, and so it aroused opposition. Before 1900 it was still possible to ignore the question and opposition had not been violent or abusive. The National Union of Women's Suffrage Societies went about its work of lobbying, and MPs were polite to it. But in innumerable ways they could hold up legislation without actually voting against it: Henry Labouchère had voted for the original John Stuart Mill amendment in favour of women in 1867 but he had grown less liberal in his opinions, and in the 1890s he amused himself by holding up bills on women's suffrage by making a long speech on the item of business immediately preceding it on the order paper. This meant that the supporters of votes for women did not even get a chance to put their case, let alone get it voted on, and it also meant that he did not have to say anything against votes for women that might infuriate the women who wanted the vote and thus increase their fighting spirit.

In 1898 the radical Dr Richard Pankhurst died and left his widow Emmeline with four children to look after, and very little money. She found a job — life would have been much harder twenty or thirty years earlier — and she was encouraged by Eva Gore-Booth and a number of other women to take an interest in politics round Manchester. In October 1903 she started the Women's Social and Political Union. 'Social' did not mean that they were going to spend their time drinking tea; the WSPU started as an ally of the Independent Labour Party, and the Pankhursts were all socialists at this stage.

In 1903 the Conservative Party had been in office for eight years, and it was beginning to lose its grip. The next election was likely to produce a Liberal government, and with a Liberal majority in the House of Commons probably most of the MPs would be fairly sympathetic

Left: The struggle becomes militant: suffragettes aggressively chain themselves to the railings of 10 Downing Street, 1908

to votes for women. Sympathy was always worth having, but it was not enough. Under the English system of government a policy that was supported by the Cabinet was practically certain to pass into law, but if the Cabinet was not interested in it, or merely thought that other things were more important, ordinary MPs would not be able to do much.

The situation was quite different from that in the United States. There the President obviously had a great deal of influence, but the individual Senators and Representatives had a great deal of freedom of action. Each one of them was worth lobbying, and each one of them was aware of the fact. The tactics of the English National Union of Women's Suffrage Societies would have made better sense in the United States; Miss Lydia Becker, the tireless and devoted secretary of the NUWSS in the 1890s, had gone round and round the MPs lobbying them in a way that would have been very useful in Washington.

The tactics of sensation-mongering

The Pankhursts understood the English system rather better; they knew that to make progress they had to arouse public opinion and make people interested in the question. They may have realised that this would arouse hostility, but hostility was more useful than indifference. In October 1905 Mrs Pankhurst's eldest daughter Christabel and Annie Kenney, a mill girl who belonged to the WSPU, were arrested and charged with trying to cause a disturbance at a political meeting in Manchester. They were found guilty and offered the choice of a small fine or imprisonment. As their overriding aim was to attract attention, naturally they chose imprisonment. And they were noticed. The newspapers of course deplored their behaviour and said that this was no way to conduct political agitation, but the press had paid so little attention to the NUWSS that all the supporters of votes for women were glad that something had been done to make people pay attention to their cause.

The general election came at the beginning of the next year, and the Liberals duly won their enormous majority. A vast crowd of enthusiastic reformers, each with his own reform to suggest, poured into the House of Commons. To be successful a reform had to catch the eye of Liberal enthusiasts without upsetting the Liberal Cabinet. The Pankhursts moved to London immediately after the election and began preparing their campaign. They began by

Right: While events in England took a spectacular, embattled turn, support for the Cause stayed, in less urbanised France, at a less impassioned level. The lithograph by Juan Gris (1910) shows the comparative calmness of a French feminist meeting

organising a procession to the Prime Minister in Downing Street, starting from Queen Boadicea's statue on the Embankment.

The Prime Minister, Sir Henry Campbell-Bannerman, listened to them politely and said he approved of votes for women, but that his Cabinet was divided on the issue. The women then went away and held a large meeting in Trafalgar Square—they were already picking up the normal methods of agitation used by men, and were soon to go rather further. They began heckling Asquith, the Chancellor of the Exchequer, at his meeting because it was well-known that he was the centre of the opposition in the Cabinet which the Prime Minister had mentioned.

The pestering of Asquith by members of the WSPU led to arrests. Annie Kenney rang at his doorbell long enough to be a nuisance, and another of the besiegers of his house slapped a policeman in the face. The women were arrested, and again chose to go to prison rather than pay their fines; there was a little argument about whether they were being properly treated in prison, though this was nothing to the commotion that broke out in a few years' time over forcible feeding.

The WSPU seemed to have succeeded in arousing public opinion. Mrs Fawcett, the leader of the NUWSS, said that the WSPU had been more successful in getting people to pay attention to the women's movement in twelve months than her own organisation had been in twelve years. Though the two organisations were still on friendly terms, the difference of approach had been noticed; the supporters of the Suffrage Societies were known as suffragists, so it was natural to call their more violent allies in the WSPU 'suffragettes'. The latter name stuck, and by now almost anyone who supported votes for women in the days before the First World War is liable to be called a suffragette. But at the time the suffragettes were a very special group—they did not always like the nickname, and sometimes called themselves 'militants'—with a special approach to politics.

It is said that Gandhi noticed what was going on in England, and was inspired by it to use methods of civil disobedience, first to help the Indians who had settled in South Africa and later, on a much larger scale, in India itself. The methods of the suffragettes suited his needs very well, just as they have suited the needs of many other agitators in other countries, working for other causes. A government which gives its people freedom to make speeches is not likely to treat them very harshly if

Left: The face of protest: arrest of an intransigent English suffragette. MPs were harangued on the terrace of the Commons from chartered river steamers by strident feminists

they break the law in a more or less symbolic way (civil disobedience in a country where the government is ruthless in using its powers would be much more risky and has not been attempted).

The political prospects for women looked a little better by the opening years of the 20th century. The transition of the six states of Australia into the Commonwealth of Australia aroused a great deal of interest in politics, and this was accompanied by a willingness to give women the vote. Women who could vote in South Australia and Western Australia were allowed to vote in federal elections from the formation of the Commonwealth in 1901, and in 1902 all women were allowed to vote in federal elections. By 1908 women in the other four states had gained complete electoral equality. This was a distinct step forward: Wyoming, or even New Zealand, might be laughed off but Australia had to be taken seriously.

The Northern democracies

In Norway something comparable happened. Norway and Sweden were still united at the beginning of the century, but the two states had a fair degree of independence in local affairs. In 1901 Norway gave the vote in municipal elections to women on a property qualification. By itself this might not have been very important, but in 1905 Norway separated from Sweden.

The new country of Norway gave some women the vote almost immediately, and by 1913 they had complete electoral equality with men. The Scandinavian approach to women was already more relaxed and egalitarian than that of any other countries — when Isadora Duncan visited Copenhagen in about 1907 she noticed the 'extraordinarily intelligent and happy look on the faces of the young women, striding along the streets alone and free, like boys'. In fact women in the Scandinavian countries were winning more and more of the immediate practical issues for which the vote would have been very useful, but were winning several of them without the help of the vote.

Finland had been under Russian rule, but in many ways Finns held the same attitudes as inhabitants of the other Scandinavian countries. The Finnish Women's Association was an important part of the country's life, and was one of the organisations that kept alive the idea of a separate nation. When Russia was in difficulty in 1905 during her war against Japan the Finns took advantage of the situation and gained a good deal of internal autonomy. In 1907 Finnish women got the vote — the first country in Europe to put them on the same footing as men in elections.

Perhaps the most serious issue raised in the Scandinavian countries — though not only in those countries — was

what became known as the 'endowment of motherhood'. Ellen Key, a Swedish social reformer, argued that mothers should be paid enough by the state to enable them to do their job properly. The Swedish reformers were quite explicit that their concern extended to unmarried mothers. They pointed out that the chief victims of the harsh traditional attitude of society towards unmarried mothers were the children, who had done nothing wrong. The supporters of endowment of motherhood were not certain whether an unmarried mother really had done anything wrong, but for tactical purposes and to avoid shocking public opinion more than they had to, the reformers always spoke as though she had sinned, but had sinned as the result of a generous and trusting disposition.

There was probably something in this. By the beginning of the century a really well-informed woman might know something about birth control: when the secretary of the Fabian Society in England conducted a survey of the married members around 1905 to ask them if they were deliberately limiting their families, a large majority of them replied that they were. Of course this was a group which would be relatively hard to shock; very few of them declined to answer on the grounds that these questions ought not to be talked about, though most people at the time would have felt outraged at being surveyed in this way.

Even so, it is not clear what methods the members used to limit their families; they may simply have been practising high-minded abstinence. The arrangements in the Asquith family have recently been revealed by Sir Oswald Mosley, who tells the story of how Mrs Asquith called on Lady Cynthia Mosley: 'Dear child, you must not have another baby for a long time. Henry always withdrew in time, such a noble man.' But an ordinary simple girl at the beginning of the century might not have heard of any method of birth control, and yet if she became a mother her position was desperate. The death rate among children of unmarried mothers was very high, sometimes because the frantic mother killed her child, sometimes through neglect and a certain amount of cruelty in the orphanages to which unwanted children were consigned, and sometimes from simple poverty.

The great surveys of poverty carried out in England at the end of the 19th century by men like Booth and Rowntree showed that poverty and large families often went together. Some politicians became convinced that children's allowance ought to be paid, and this view gained a good deal of support on the continent of Europe. It was a reform which appealed to right-wing politicians as well,

Left: An English suffragette appeals to an all-male audience

because it would encourage expansion of population, and make sure that young children were brought up fit and strong, both of which would be useful for the large armies, based on compulsory military service, that were maintained in Europe. The idea was less successful in the English-speaking world; England and Canada waited until the end of the Second World War before introducing family allowances, and the United States has never accepted the idea. Anyway, these allowances have been intended to supplement the husband's wage and make it easier to bring up a large family. The idea that a mother had a right to receive payments large enough to enable her to bring up a family by herself is still more revolutionary.

H.G.Wells and the female heart

While the argument about 'the endowment of motherhood' was on, H.G.Wells wrote his political novel *The New Machiavelli*. It is remembered today for its venomous account of the home life, the meagre hospitality, and the unceasing political intrigues of Sidney and Beatrice Webb; and it was intended as a tract in favour of generous payments to mothers and attacking the institution of marriage. Wells in his personal life showed an inability to confine himself within the strict bounds of marriage – apparently one of the humorous sights at literary and political conferences in the 1920s was to see Wells with his close friend, the Baroness Budberg, hurrying along behind him – and in the context of the pre-1914 world he was seen as a liberating influence.

Bernard Shaw at the end of his play *Pygmalion* tidies some of his characters out of the story by explaining that they came across H.G.Wells and immediately all their social problems were solved. Not Eliza Doolittle's problems of course, which were only to be solved by a magnetic teacher with no real interest in women, which was basically Shaw's idea of himself; but the other, more middle-class young women in the play were, as Shaw realised, more suited for Wells's prescription than anything he could suggest.

Wells's novel *Ann Veronica* (autobiographical in its later chapters) may have convinced Shaw that Wells understood this particular problem. Ann Veronica was just the sort of girl to become a young and active suffragette; educated to do a job, working in a scientific laboratory, frustrated by the fact that her parents seem not to understand why she is so fidgety and anxious to go out into the world. The novel gave, among other things, a pen-portrait of Christabel Pankhurst and an account of imprisonment after a demonstration. But Wells was writing a romance rather than a political novel – there seem

to be no worthwhile novels about the suffragettes – and in the end Ann Veronica got her slice of real life by going off to live with a married man. The story had a happy ending; the man's wife disappeared and he and Ann married, to the intense and understandable relief of her parents.

Only a small number of people became suffragettes and broke the law or struggled with the police. The strength of the suffragettes depended on the fact that they had an army of supporters behind them who approved of votes for women – some of them girls suffering from Ann Veronica's type of frustration, but many older people as well. Some of their supporters regretted their methods, but their form of active agitation did not cost the cause any supporters for the first four or five years in which they were used.

Asquith – a formidable opponent

Advocates of votes for women suffered a nasty setback at the beginning of 1908. Campbell-Bannerman, a passive friend, retired from the premiership, and died almost immediately. His successor was Asquith, with his memories of being badgered by the suffragettes in the previous years. Asquith was too cautious a man, and altogether too skilful a politician, to talk about his reasons for opposing votes for women. His second wife, Margot, was brilliant but erratically clever; after he had been forced out of the premiership in 1916 she published her autobiography, which harmed him in his efforts to get back into power. Among other things it suggested that the Asquiths went on opposing votes for women even after the law giving them the vote had been passed.

Asquith was fond of his wife, but was quite unlike her. He had a neat turn of phrase, though he did not always use it in a way to win him friends. He once said, 'I am sometimes tempted to think, as one listens to the arguments of supporters of woman suffrage, that there is nothing to be said for it, and I am sometimes tempted to think, when I listen to the arguments of the opponents of woman suffrage, that there is nothing to be said against it': neither side can have been pleased by this assessment of the situation, though the opponents of change did have the satisfaction of knowing that Asquith was helping their side.

But the forces against him were impressive. The more

Left: A gallery of the first women lawyers (late 19th century).
Left from top to bottom: Marie Popelin (Belgium), Signé Silen (Finland), Jeanne Chauvin (France), Nanna Berg (Denmark).
Right from top to bottom: Four Americans – Clara Shortridge Foltz, Florence Cronise, Mary Greene, and Belva Lockwood

peaceful supporters of votes for women had organised a march in February 1907 — owing to the rain it became known as the 'Mud March' — in which about 4,000 people took part. Male helpers were called in to help: the rising economist Maynard Keynes acted as a steward, and the rising literary man Lytton Strachey ought to have been there but hurried away to Cambridge out of a feeling that he might be going to make a fool of himself.

Three days later the less peaceful suffragettes held a march. The procession was broken up by mounted policemen, who rode the women down with some ferocity. The London press could not take the suffragettes seriously, but it protested very firmly against this use of the police. The government began to be worried: it could not agree on a policy about votes for women, but it realised that clashes between women and the police, whether they did good or harm to the women's cause, could only damage the prestige and electoral position of the government. This thought was to trouble the government quite often in the next few years, but they found no solution to the problem.

Top right: Norway — matriculation of the first female student at Christiania University, 1882. **Bottom:** Finland — pressure from the Finnish Women's Association results in electoral equality for women, 1907: the first European country to achieve it

'The Screaming Sisterhood'

As a stirring topical theme, 'Votes for Women' was meat and drink to the cartoonist. That woman is always news is an old journalistic truth, but, now that she had become a natural subject for parody, caricature, and crusading idealism, the pencil became for a while mightier than the pen. **Below:** Many thought that an attractive woman was her own best spokesman and that femininity was enough. *Punch* magazine promoted the myth that 'women who wanted women's rights also wanted women's charms', that only the gauche and the ugly needed the artificial support of votes. **Top right:** Lloyd George's 'mewing cats'. The truculence of the suffragettes aroused deep masculine prejudices and fears of the danger of 'sacrificing one's manhood'. **Bottom right:** A poster issued by the Women's Social and Political Union: the logic seemed impeccable, but the consequences unforeseeable. Politicians equivocated and played uneasily for time. Nobody knew how women would vote.

AS THEY DRI
THERE WERE
AND THE BO
FOR A TIME

...HEIR PATH
...OF 'VOTES' OR 'DEATH'
...LD HIS BREATH

THE PEOPLE NOT THE COMMONS MUST DECIDE ...E TAXES

WOMEN ARE HALF THE PEOPLE & DEMAND A VOICE IN DECIDING THE TAXES

THE COMMONS AS REPRESETATIVES OF THE PEOPLE MUST DECIDE THE TAXES

A. PATRIO

Chapter 5
The Advance of the Suffragettes

The opponents of votes for women did have one advantage, apart from Asquith's support. In England (as in the United States) votes for women could not be passed into law without affecting the rest of the political situation. In the United States there was the question of prohibition, and the fear of everybody in the liquor trade that if women had the vote they would ruin the trade. There was also the fear of the southern whites that if women got the vote it would be harder to keep a grip on the southern Negroes. Enough southerners remembered the explosive effect of Harriot Beecher Stowe's *Uncle Tom's Cabin* in arousing support for abolition of slavery to know that northern women were powerful and determined, and were remarkably hard to persuade that Negroes were getting a fair deal. In addition, there was the point of view expressed by the southern Senator who said that he reckoned they could always hit a Negro man on the head if he tried to vote, but he was not so sure that hitting Negro women would be acceptable.

The cross-currents in England were not so bitter, but they did hold up the pressure for change. The difficulty was that only about two-thirds of the men in England had the vote: only a householder could be a voter, and men who lived with their parents, or who lived in ordinary rented rooms or flats did not have the right to vote. Perhaps this should have consoled the women for being excluded, but its actual effect was to make it less likely that women would get the vote.

One simple proposal was to give the vote to everybody, man or woman, at the age of twenty-one. But the proposal was altogether too simple: no Conservative, whether he belonged to the pro-votes for women minority in the Conservative Party or not, wanted to see so many poor people added to the voters' list. The Conservative supporters of votes for women wanted to restrict the vote to women householders, and of course in practically every

Left: The Executive Committee of the International Council for Women meeting in July 1899: Susan Brownell Anthony, the American suffrage leader, is second from left in the front row

family the man was the householder. The Conservative approach would have given the vote to a small group made up of widows and spinsters of wealthy families (and, it was pointed out, to the more successful prostitutes who had acquired houses of their own, though there cannot have been many of them). The Liberals did not like this idea at all.

The women themselves did not really mind, at this stage, what approach was taken. They wanted to get some women on to the voters' list, and calculated that the rest would probably follow. If it had to be a limited Conservative-type franchise, they would put up with it. However, at this point the women in the WSPU were divided by an argument within their organisation which had very little to do with suffragette principles or tactics. Policy in the Union was controlled by the emergency committee, and the emergency committee was dominated by Mrs Pankhurst and her two daughters Christabel and Sylvia. They were the core of the movement, and would have dominated the Union whatever the constitution said, but some members challenged their authority and tried to make the committee more directly responsible to the membership.

A remarkable family

Mrs Pankhurst was a lady, and a lady of immense determination, considerable skill in speaking and in propaganda, and (as became clear later) no regard for her health, her safety, or her life itself, if they had to be sacrificed for the cause. Christabel was a convincing answer to anyone who thought the suffragettes were dull or dowdy. She was very obviously good-looking, she had immense vitality, she had her mother's skill as a speaker; it was not quite so clear that she was a lady. Sylvia was fairly certainly not a lady. At first she wanted to be an art student and then she became convinced that something would have to be done for the poor. Because she was a Pankhurst she was a suffragette, but she was one of the few members of the WSPU who remembered that it had started off as a socialist organisation and felt that it ought not to become a feminist group with no other political commitments. This caused trouble later, but in the first of the WSPU's internal struggles she was firmly on her mother's side.

Mrs Pankhurst could probably have won the majority of the members to her side if she had asked for their support in the normal way. Instead she carried out a coup, seized control of the organisation, and imposed a new constitution. None of the suffragettes were meek and

Right: Sylvia Pankhurst speaking in the East End of London

mild, and those who were not devoted admirers of Mrs Pankhurst would not stand for such behaviour. They set up the Women's Freedom League; the main difference between it and the Pankhurst-dominated WSPU was that it did not believe in violence, but its members were quite ready to break the law by holding processions in defiance of the police and by refusing to pay taxes.

One great difference between the WSPU and all the other women's organisations was that Mrs Pankhurst had got her teeth into London and meant to stay there. The other organisations were strong all over the country; the WSPU was concentrated in London, and most of its violent and vigorous steps to publicise its cause were taken in London. This made sense; the suffragettes lived by publicity, and they wanted to gain the attention of the press. The British press was dominated by the London newspapers, and if the newspaper reported that a suffragette meeting had been broken up by the police in London, the whole country would soon hear about it. Comparable meetings anywhere else in the country would receive much less attention.

People at the time — especially Asquith and the opponents of votes for women — knew perfectly well what was going on. They also knew that the antics in London mattered only if they aroused enthusiasm outside London. A Miss New chained herself to the railings in Downing Street and started shouting 'Votes for Women' while a Cabinet meeting was going on. Until the police brought a hacksaw to cut the chains she went on shouting, and attracting so much attention that Mrs Drummond, one of Mrs Pankhurst's trusted lieutenants, was able to get into 10 Downing Street and shout 'Votes for Women' inside the Prime Minister's own house.

This sort of thing would not convince the anti-suffrage ministers but — apart from being great fun — it did attract the attention of other women and make them interested in the struggle. Miss Matters, of the Women's Freedom League, chartered a balloon and flew across London, dropping leaflets on the way: perhaps some of the leaflets reached the people who read them and were convinced, but the flight made sure that nobody could forget about the suffragettes. Some women tried presenting a petition to Edward VII when he was going to open Parliament; perhaps they thought he had some influence on these political questions, but the main point was to provide a public demonstration.

In the summer of 1908 larger processions were held than in 1907 — and in better weather. In June the suffrage

Right: Mrs Charlotte Despard, socialist and pacifist chairman of the Women's Freedom League, speaking in Trafalgar Square

societies held a combined procession from the Embankment to the Albert Hall. They came in groups, artists, actresses, graduates, and writers, each carrying an embroidered banner to say who they were. Mrs Pankhurst led one section, the Women's Freedom League marched as another section, and the movement appeared united and harmonious.

The next weekend the WSPU put on a demonstration of its own: an open-air meeting at Hyde Park, at which it marked itself off from the other suffrage societies by adding a purple stripe to the white and green colours adopted by all supporters of votes for women. Special trains brought supporters to London, and *The Times* estimated that over 500,000 people came to the meeting — an improbably large number (for comparison, the Campaign for Nuclear Disarmament on some occasions got a crowd in the order of 100,000 to Trafalgar Square and the great civil rights demonstration in Washington in the summer of 1963, at which Martin Luther King made his 'I have a dream' speech, was estimated at about 250,000 people).

But even if the suffragette meeting was not as large as *The Times* said, it was still a distinct demonstration of their importance. And the government presented them a few weeks later with another opportunity to gain publicity. Mrs Pankhurst, Christabel, and Mrs Drummond were put on trial for conduct likely to provoke a breach of the peace at a meeting in Trafalgar Square. The three women were convicted, and were sent to prison after they refused to promise not to commit a breach of the peace again. Such a promise would probably have stopped them from organising any more meetings, so it was hardly likely that they would give it.

The campaign hots up

By 1909 it could be seen that there would be a general election, after the House of Lords had rejected the government's budget. Politics naturally became livelier, and the methods of the suffragettes became livelier to meet the occasion. When the Prime Minister went to Birmingham, his organisers found to their dismay that the only really large meeting-hall in the city had a glass roof; they rigged up a tarpaulin across it and when two women climbed up to the roof they were arrested before they could **69** ▷

Top right: Militancy provokes arrest after a scuffle round Nelson's Column. Bottom: Suffragettes march in their white 'injured innocence' dresses. Sylvia Pankhurst, aloft, leads the chanting. Next page: 'The Haunted House': a contemporary poster shows the House of Commons lying uneasily beneath the heavy, brooding and unwelcome menace of 'Votes for Women'

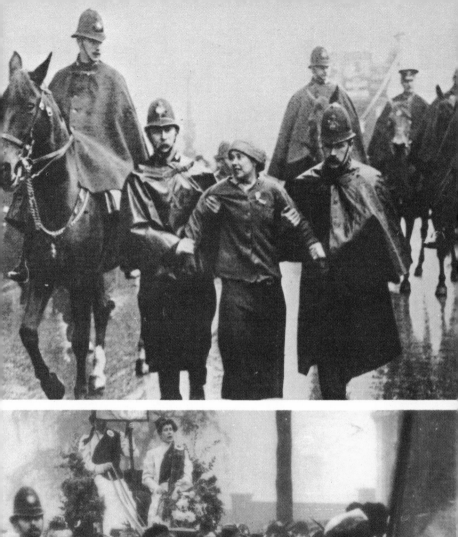

THE HAUNTED HOUSE

smash the glass. Another woman tried to attack Winston Churchill with a dog-whip though he managed to take it away from her before she could injure him.

Women hid under the platform at meetings (and at the Albert Hall inside the organ) and jumped out shouting 'Votes for Women'; they continued to arrange large processions; and one woman locked herself into Lloyd George's car and gave him a long harangue on the importance of giving women the vote. But although the suffragettes had no reason to feel friendly to the Liberal government, they knew that a much larger proportion of the Conservative opposition was hostile to votes for women.

Hunger strikes
The government did not face the situation with equal satisfaction. Keeping the suffragettes in order became harder in 1909 when women in prison started going on hunger strike. At first any woman who seemed to be growing weak during a hunger strike was released. But this was too easy: any woman who had departed far enough from the conventions of the age to get arrested for a political demonstration was probably determined enough to go on hunger strike, and a policy of rapid release simply meant that all prison sentences would be reduced to a matter of three or four days. And the government would look very silly.

So the government had to proceed to forcible feeding. No British government could like this, especially a Liberal government which depended on Irish support. Some of the Irish MPs had themselves been in prison in the 1880s for political offences and several of them were sensitive about prison conditions. In any case this was a period of growing concern about prison conditions. Churchill, who was Home Secretary at this time, was particularly sensitive to charges that women prisoners were ill-treated. The story was told that he wanted to be quite sure that forcible feeding was as humane as his civil servants told him, and accordingly he arranged to be fed forcibly himself.

If the government was finding the struggle a little wearing, some members of the House of Commons were determined to bring it to an end in the only complete and final way, by passing an act giving women the vote. In 1910 a Conciliation Committee was formed, with members drawn from all parties, to produce a bill which could bring together all supporters of votes for women.

The bill they produced was an almost complete acceptance of the Conservative point of view, giving the vote to

Left: A suffragist poster pleads for an end to men's paternalism

women householders, including women who owned a piece of property which was not being used as her husband's qualification for voting. This meant that apart from the widows and spinsters (and perhaps prostitutes) who would benefit if women householders got the vote, the bill would also give votes to wives whose husbands had two homes. Naturally people rich enough to keep up two addresses usually voted Conservative rather than Liberal.

Lloyd George and Churchill opposed this particular bill on the grounds that it gave too much to the Conservatives, though they stressed their commitment to the principle. The debate was enlivened by Lord Hugh Cecil's statement that when voting 'I am not conscious of performing a function either difficult or sensational or particularly masculine. . . . It is a serenely tranquil, an austerely refined, and from beginning to end a thoroughly ladylike operation.' The bill got a majority on the second reading, but clearly was not going to get any further.

Deadlock had also appeared in national politics. Another election about the House of Lords had to be held in December 1910, and in this election Asquith softened enough to say that if the Liberals won the election they would produce a bill to widen the franchise. The more optimistic supporters of votes for women saw this as a virtual promise that they would get their way and that Asquith would withdraw as gracefully as he could. The election made little difference to the parties in the House of Commons, the Liberals remained in office, and early in 1911 the WSPU called off the campaign of agitation by violence. Peace and the hope of a reasonable settlement dawned in England, and Mrs Pankhurst went to North America to tell the story of the struggle.

Top right: Suffragettes freshly released from prison often retired to Eagle House, Bath, to recuperate. For everyone who stayed there a tree was planted in a special arboretum. Here Mrs Pankhurst *(right)* and Annie Kenney *(left)* pause for a break; Mary Blathwayt, the owner's daughter, is in the centre.
Bottom: Stirring times for the feminist vanguard in America

Chapter 6
Regrouping in the United States

The American suffrage societies had healed their quarrel over Victoria Woodhull, and in 1890 had formed the National American Woman Suffrage Association. But they had not done much more than this. In a country as large as the United States, with a federal constitution, organisation and co-ordination were vital; and they were nowhere to be found. In the four western states which had given women the vote, quite apart from the lack of servants or of a strong liquor interest, there were simply very few people to be canvassed; in the larger states the population was too large for the women's organisations to have much effect.

Some of the American suffrage leaders thought the best line of approach was to get Congress to initiate a constitutional amendment. Susan B. Anthony, the second president of the reunited NAWSA, was committed to this method; in the course of years the proposal became known as the Susan B. Anthony amendment, and eventually the form of words she suggested in 1875 was adopted forty-five years later. Because of the risk that the measure would get lost in the intricacies of Congressional procedure another group of leaders preferred to press the individual state legislatures which controlled voter qualifications. But a change on this scale often required a referendum to change the state constitution, and so the women who thought they could get the vote through the individual states found themselves plodding through a succession of campaigns that needed a great deal of organisation.

When Susan Anthony retired in 1900 she chose a woman a whole generation younger than herself to be the new leader of the NAWSA. Mrs Carrie Chapman Catt was ideally suited for the task of reducing the United States to a series of neatly indexed cards listing people who would work for votes for women, Senators and Representatives who would support it, people who could be **77** ▷

77 ▷

Left: Campaigning for women's suffrage in the USA. The bystanders show amused tolerance. Next page: NAWSA, presided over by George Washington, prepares for the dawn

NATIONAL·AMERICAN·WOMAN

28

ANNUAL CONV

ELIZABETH CADY STANTON

THE WOMAN'S BIBLE

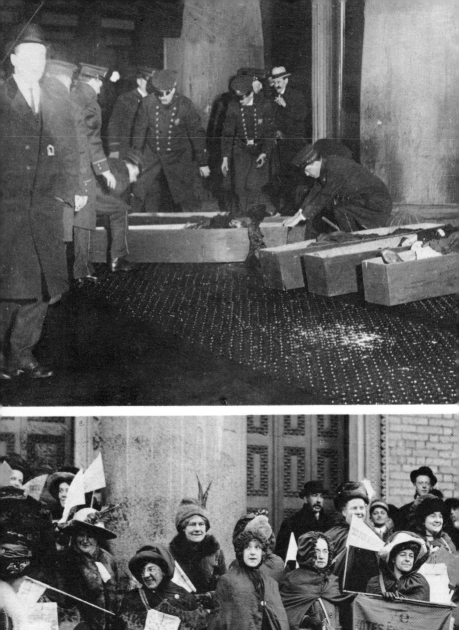

organised to help, and people whose opposition would have to be met and overcome. This operation was necessary but not exciting; after she had spent four years making the machinery efficient she retired, to be replaced by Dr Anne Shaw who was an inspiring orator, a less efficient organiser, and a dozen years older than Mrs Catt.

Dr Anne Shaw did not do much better than Mrs Catt. The question looked dead in 1900, and for another decade no progress was made. But Mrs Pankhurst's visit in 1911 came at a moment of great hope and change; between 1910 and 1912 another six states gave women the vote by referendum. All ten women's suffrage states were in the west, all of them except California were inclined to be dry, and most of them either had a state-wide Prohibition law or passed one in the next few years.

Cautious advance

The women could not hope for much progress in the south. The southern ideal of a lady made no allowances for her taking part in politics, and southerners had no desire to see anyone extending the franchise at any time. So the women had to concentrate on the cities of the east if they were to make any progress. The women who wanted the vote were inevitably middle-class and almost equally inevitably Anglo-Saxon. They were also inclined to dislike Negroes and immigrants, because Negroes and immigrants were the backbone of the strength of the machine politicians and the machine politicians were usually against giving women the vote. The attitude of the party machine was shown in Illinois in 1913: the legislature allowed women to vote for the President of the United States, but did not allow them to vote for Congress or for state office; and, of course, the reason was that the machine was not much worried about Presidential elections, but was concerned about the less important positions.

New York was an even harder proposition than Illinois. A Women's Suffrage Party had been launched there, and it made some progress by taking a liberal line on questions of social reform. Votes for women received a great forward thrust from the Triangle Fire in 1911; an unsafe building, full of badly-paid garment workers, caught fire and 146 of the workers were burnt to death or killed when they jumped from the upper floors. Opponents of votes for women pointed out that there were many unsafe buildings in New York in which men might be burnt to death even though they had the vote, but the fire

*Top left: The aftermath of the Triangle Shirt Fire, 1911, which aroused widespread sympathy for reform. **Bottom left:** Suffrage 'hikers', 1913: staunchly respectable pilgrims spread the Cause*

77

aroused interest in a wide range of reforms and women's suffrage benefited along with the others.

The great parades

Some of this enthusiasm showed itself in the form of great parades. New York, and American cities in general, were more accustomed to parades and marching organisations than English cities, but the New York parades in 1912 were spectacular enough to attract attention from the most jaded audience. People came to jeer, but on the whole the city was tolerant enough and in any case the marchers were obviously highly respectable and were well-ordered and well-dressed; the whole thing was very reminiscent of elegant marches with embroidered banners in London half-a-dozen years earlier. Women picketed the party conventions that year, and arranged parades in several cities.

A parade in Washington was organised in March 1913 when President Wilson was inaugurated, and the orderly, tidy procession began its march. But it was held up by an anti-suffrage mob, and the police (who had given a permit for the march) made very little effort to help it go on. The riot that followed had the effect that might be expected: the women had been badly treated, and a great many people who had come to Washington for the inauguration had seen that they had been badly treated. Sympathy for the women turned into support for giving votes to women.

The 1913 riot in Washington, and the reaction in favour of women, was a great encouragement to American women who wanted to show that they too could fight for the vote. Mrs Pankhurst's visit had been at a time of truce in England; by 1913 the struggle in England was raging much more fiercely than ever before, and this inflamed the struggle in the United States as well. Two young Americans who had been working with the suffragettes in England, Alice Paul and Lucy Burns, rapidly rose to positions of importance after they came back to the United States; they controlled the Congressional Committee of the NAWSA and at the same time they launched their own Congressional Union — as the names suggest, they were firmly committed to making progress through Congress and forcing it to accept the Susan Anthony amendment to the constitution.

They believed that the methods of the suffragettes could be transplanted across the Atlantic and used in Washington. Perhaps they were right, but the NAWSA certainly did not think so; the sensational approach might

Right: The gathering momentum: suffragette parades in Washington (top) and Greenwich Village, New York (bottom) 1913

78

be all very well in England, but in America respectability should be the keynote of the campaign. Within the year Miss Paul and Miss Burns had been pushed out of the Congressional Committee, and Dr Shaw's position as President was weakened because she had supported the two newcomers.

But the pair of them still had their Congressional Union, and it quickly became the American equivalent of the WSPU. Mrs Belmont, one of the wealthiest women in the United States, supported it with her money, partly because her ex-husband William Vanderbilt opposed votes for women. It quickly took the name of the Women's Party and by 1915 it was organising groups throughout the country. But the NAWSA had no intention of being pushed aside; it quickly reorganised itself, Dr Shaw retired from the Presidency and was replaced by Mrs Catt, which showed that the members felt that stricter discipline and less oratorical inspiration were needed.

Despite the NAWSA's efforts to revitalise itself, in 1916 the Women's Party was certainly succeeding in attracting attention. Apart from parades and struggles with the police, they began picketing the White House. President Wilson was understood to be favourable to votes for women, and at first he smiled politely and raised his hat. But the suffragettes went on to chain themselves to his railings; this was not as effective as in Downing Street, because there is a large and pleasant lawn between the railings and the White House, but it still showed that the suffragettes were determined to attract attention.

Even so, their demonstrations in the United States never reached the level of raw fury seen in England in the years immediately before 1914. The Women's Party upset the NAWSA; and naturally a good many people who wanted to escape the polite lobbying of the NAWSA would assure the ladies who visited them that it was all the fault of the suffragettes who were making such a fuss – the NAWSA always took refusals of this sort at face value, and blamed the Women's Party, but probably a good many of the people who gave this excuse were implacable enemies of votes for women who did not want to publicise the fact.

Left: *Mrs Emmeline Pankhurst seated in front of Mrs Belfont, the New York suffrage leader. The Cause attracted supporters from rich high society* **(top left)**, *and even the men got in on the act with a League for Women Suffrage, in New York* **(bottom)**

Chapter 7
The Struggle in England Resumes

The situation in England, which had looked peaceful and likely to end quietly when Mrs Pankhurst visited North America in 1911, had slipped out of control quite quickly. The first step came in November 1911 when Asquith announced that his government was just about to introduce a bill that would give votes to all adults, and he said that amendments to give votes to women would be discussed. If the Commons voted for them, the government would not make any difficulties.

Mrs Pankhurst, still in North America, denounced this as treachery, which must have looked like an unnecessary willingness to resist any attempt at conciliation. The suffragettes opposed the government's approach because the fiercer members of the WSPU wanted a separate act of Parliament giving women the vote, and did not want to be enfranchised simply as an afterthought in a bill primarily concerned with giving more men the vote.

Mounting violence
The difference between giving women the vote in a bill which was all their own and lumping them in with the men started the whole struggle off again. Before Mrs Pankhurst had got back to England from North America there was a great scuffle between the police and a procession of suffragettes in Parliament Square – 200 women were arrested. When Mrs Pankhurst did get back she invited her followers at a mass meeting to go out and break windows: 'We don't want to use any arguments that are unnecessarily strong. If the argument of the stone, the time-honoured official political argument, is sufficient, then we will never use any stronger argument.'

Before this threatened escalation took place, there was another and more violent – almost final – quarrel between the suffragists and the suffragettes. A large and respectable meeting of suffragists was held in the Albert Hall, with Lloyd George as the main speaker and Mrs Fawcett the suffragist leader as chairman. The suffragettes came

Left: Lady chauffeur in Downing Street demonstration, 1911

and shouted at him and called him a traitor, and although the meeting was not broken up it was harder for suffragists to feel sympathy for the suffragettes afterwards.

A week later Mrs Pankhurst's notion of an official political argument was put into effect. At four o'clock in the afternoon of 1st March 1912 a well-disciplined group of 200 women broke most of the windows in the smart shopping area round Piccadilly Circus and along Regent Street and Oxford Street; some of them brought bags of stones for this, and the better-equipped had come with hammers so that they could go on attacking several panes one after another. Mrs Pankhurst herself went to Downing Street to throw stones – not a sensible arrangement, for she was a notoriously bad shot.

The 200 window-breakers were arrested, and the government also decided to arrest the other WSPU leaders. Christabel heard that the police were coming and left quickly for Paris, but Mr and Mrs Pethick-Lawrence, two other prominent WSPU members, were arrested at the WSPU headquarters in Clement's Inn – not a tavern but one of the elegant lodging-places for lawyers and professional people near the Law Courts.

Leadership divisions
Mr Pethick-Lawrence (later Lord Pethick-Lawrence, a Labour peer) was one of the few men to play an active part at any stage in the women's agitation. Many husbands were willing and eager to support their wives in their actions, and several politicians were ready to speak on behalf of votes for women, but very little of the organising work in the movement was done by men. Most of the campaigns waged to give the right to vote to people who were previously unenfranchised have been led by enthusiasts who already have the vote, as in the struggles for the successive Reform Bills in 19th-century England, and in the struggles to get Negroes the vote in the United States. But the women did all their own organising, as pictures of committees and conferences will show. Mr Pethick-Lawrence's position, as the treasurer and fundraiser of an extremist society, was unique. The WSPU was very good at raising money and had a substantial balance at the bank, as was proved at the trial of the leaders. It put out its magazine, *Votes for Women,* and paid the expenses of a number of full-time organisers. Its militant and aggressive policy does not seem to have frightened away subscribers, and probably attracted people to give money by being the organisation that was most visibly fighting to get the vote.

The three leaders were sentenced to nine months in prison, and although the sentences were shortened as

much as possible – partly because they went on hunger strike – this interval gave them time to reconsider their position. For the parliamentary situation had changed, in an ominous direction. A month after the window-breaking demonstration the House of Commons rejected a more wide-ranging version of the Conciliation Bill which had been dropped in 1910. The upholders of respectable lobbying and discreet pressure said that this defeat showed that window-breaking cost the cause votes where they really mattered. The admirers of the suffragettes claimed (and claim to this day) that the bill was defeated for quite different reasons: they pointed out that the Irish MPs had changed their minds and voted against the bill, presumably because they thought it might complicate the parliamentary timetable and hinder their darling project of Home Rule for Ireland; and that some MPs preferred to wait for Asquith's bill to give votes to all men to be discussed, because they understood it could be amended to include women as well.

While the Pethick-Lawrences and Mrs Pankhurst were in prison, the campaign was run from Paris by Christabel. The faithful Annie Kenney, who had been in the militant movement from the beginning, slipped across the Channel to see her every week and picked up instructions for the next move.

The swing to extremism

When the imprisoned leaders came out, the results of their meditations could soon be seen. The Pethick-Lawrences suggested that the suffragettes should not go any further in attacking property; Mrs Pankhurst obviously disagreed, and soon showed that she wanted the movement to go in for arson. She expelled the Pethick-Lawrences from the WSPU on her own authority and announced that she and Christabel would now be the sole leaders; the Pethick-Lawrences, who had been editing *Votes for Women,* kept their paper but Christabel launched a new and more militant paper, *The Suffragette.* The expulsion of the Pethick-Lawrences was much more amicable than the expulsion of the Women's Freedom League leaders five years previously, but the suffragettes were still to be regarded as a military movement, and the commands of the leader were to be obeyed without discussion.

This was an odd attitude for the leaders of a political agitation to take, but then the whole 'atmosphere of discussion was becoming very odd. Sir Almroth Wright, a

Left: *Forcible feeding of a 'hunger striker'. At least one prisoner was driven insane by the methods used: a tube was thrust up the nostrils by one doctor and food poured down it by another*

doctor of some distinction, wrote a very peculiar letter to *The Times:* he suggested that half the women in the country went mad to some extent as a result of the menopause, and he made it clear that he regarded militancy as a symptom of mental illness. He wrote: 'There are no good women, but only women who have lived under the influence of good men.' And he said that some of the suffragettes had a programme which was 'licence for themselves or else restriction for men'.

The suffragettes did not put the question quite like that. Some wanted restriction; some wanted licence. In *The Suffragette* Christabel Pankhurst wrote a series of articles on venereal disease, later published as a book, *The Great Scourge.* By the standards of the time it was undoubtedly outspoken; but venereal disease was a menace, and Christabel was doing a service to the community in pointing it out. During the First World War, when the wastage of men owing to disease was reducing the effectiveness of the army, the book was reprinted as a guide and a warning. Although she blamed the strict sexual morality of the time and the consequent resort to prostitutes for much of the trouble, she made it clear that she was not advocating free love or any anticipation of marriage. As she put it in the introduction, the programme was 'Votes for Women and Chastity for Men', a much more elevated attitude than the one attributed to the suffragettes by Sir Almroth Wright. Votes for women, in Christabel's idea of the future, would lead to a strict enforcement of the laws against prostitution by punishing the men who went to prostitutes as well as the women themselves.

The insistence on chastity for men was not just a question of dealing with venereal disease. The 'double standard' of morality, which laid down that sex outside marriage was a trivial indulgence for men, and perhaps a sign of virility as well, while it was an indelible disgrace for women, was a clear sign of the inequality of the sexes and the way that women's position was inferior. Christabel's approach was stern and puritanical; on the more extreme fringes of the women's movement was a magazine called *The Freewoman* which was committed to the freer varieties of free love. 'To the healthy human being there is something repugnant in long-continued sexual relationship with a person with whom one is in the constant and often jarring intimacy of daily life' and 'I repeat that sterilisation is a higher human achievement than reproduction' must have left the respectable Miss Pankhurst feeling that the suffragette cause had quite enough difficulties already without getting mixed up with views like this.

The opponents of votes for women also had their ex-

tremists. Mrs Humphrey Ward, the anti-suffragist leader, felt she had to apologise for Sir Almroth Wright's letter (which, of course, had had the effect of convincing a good many women that the suffragettes were right). People had been saying odd things about women for a good many years: Lombroso, one of the earliest criminologists, had said 'even the normal woman is a half-criminaloid being' and the *Saturday Review* had called educated women 'vermin'. But there was now an increase in the number of odd things said.

Support from the Labour Party

With people in this sort of mood they were not likely to reach a friendly compromise at all easily. The struggle was growing more heated when George Lansbury, a Labour MP, became convinced that the government's treatment of women was intolerable. The Labour Party had about forty MPs at the time, most of them committed to votes for women. In 1912 the party conference laid down that no extension of the right to vote would be acceptable unless it gave votes to women — a startling commitment, because the Parliamentary Labour Party would be committed to opposing the government's forthcoming bill and resisting the efforts of the Liberals to enfranchise just that section of the population which would be most likely to vote Labour unless the bill included votes for women. So the Labour Party had arranged for itself a position where it might eventually be obliged to do its best to cut its own throat.

Lansbury however was no man for delay: he went out to cut his own throat immediately. He denounced the Prime Minister in the Commons: 'You are torturing innocent women.' Then in November 1912 he resigned his seat and stood again at the by-election as a women's suffrage candidate. In 1910 he had been elected by the efforts of the local Labour Party organisation, helped by the Liberals putting forward no candidate; at the by-election in 1912 some of his Labour supporters saw no need for a new election and the others got on badly with the WSPU.

The suffragettes felt that, as he was standing for their cause, they should run the whole campaign, but naturally they did not know the East End constituency of Bromley and Bow which he represented. If the suffragettes had worked with the existing organisation, Lans-

Top left: The apprehensive wait before final release. **Centre and bottom:** *A French view of feminists in operation — in England, hounding ministers* **(centre right)**; *in Germany, speechifying* **(centre left)**; *in Russia, terrorising* **(bottom left)**; *in France, most successfully, wearing the trousers* **(bottom right)**

bury might have won. As it was, his supporters did not get on together, and right at the end the WSPU motorcars were not made available to bring known Labour voters to the polling stations. Lansbury was defeated and the cause of votes for women suffered, though all that the defeat really showed was that the WSPU and the Labour Party did not have much in common. Sylvia Pankhurst believed in socialist principles, and stayed on in the East End, but the main body of the suffragettes went away convinced that an alliance with the Conservatives would be a good idea. And the suffragette hostility to legislation to give votes to poorer men — because they wanted women to have a bill all to themselves — looked like a pro-Conservative attitude.

Asquith's betrayal?

But at last in January 1913 Asquith's bill to give votes to all men was to be debated, and the supporters of votes for women prepared a series of amendments to put women in the bill. There was a day of debate on the women's suffrage amendments; some Cabinet Ministers spoke for the change, others spoke against, for the issue was treated as an open question, in the way that capital punishment has been treated at Westminster in more recent years. Next day the Prime Minister asked the Speaker what would be the effect on the bill if an amendment giving votes to women was passed. The Speaker then gave his ruling: the bill was supposed to be to give votes to men, and if the women were brought in, the amendment would be so fundamental that the whole structure of the bill would have been overturned. Accordingly, if the women's amendments were passed, an entirely new bill would have to be introduced.

Asquith said politely that the government's bill and the promise that amendments could be introduced had been based on a misunderstanding; the government would withdraw its bill. Asquith said that there had been no sharp practice but inevitably the suffragettes did not believe him and they were convinced that he had known all along what the Speaker would do.

Within the women's movement the effect of the fiasco was to strengthen the position of the Pankhursts. They had cried out for no compromise and no amendments, they had said that the government was not to be trusted and was no true friend of votes for women, and they had been proved right. The WSPU attracted supporters away from the decorous constitutional societies which had believed in the good faith of the government. The Pethick-Lawrences appeared as weak-kneed in their opposition to a drastic policy. The next step up from breaking windows was — it had always been obvious — for the suffra-

gettes to turn to arson. And in the early months of 1913 they did just that.

Arrests for arson

They burnt a couple of rural railway stations, they placed a bomb in the house being built for Lloyd George at Walton Heath in Surrey, and they wrote 'Votes for Women' in acid on the greens of some golf courses. And these attacks were meant to hurt; previously women who had been breaking the law, whether in a peaceful way by marching in a procession without police permission, or violently by breaking windows or trying to force their way into the Commons, had intended to be arrested in order to show that they took their beliefs seriously, and to make a speech from the dock in defence of their beliefs at the trial. But by this stage the suffragettes were no longer looking for opportunities for martyrdom. They wanted to fight against society.

They were sometimes caught by the police, and in any case there were still some less violent demonstrators trying to get arrested in what had been the normal way. The government took fresh powers to deal with the problem caused by hunger-striking; the 'Cat-and-Mouse' Act allowed the Home Secretary to release any prisoner who had gone on hunger strike, but then to bring her back to complete her sentence when she had recovered her health. Naturally the mice declined to co-operate; once a hunger-striker was out of prison she usually tried to elude the police. Mrs Pankhurst was something of an exception; she was constantly being rearrested under the 'Cat-and-Mouse' Act, and as constantly being released because she had been reduced by her unceasing efforts to a state of weakness where a day or two on hunger-strike made it necessary to release her. The government was naturally terrified that she would die; it would be worse if she died in prison, but if she died anywhere the government would be blamed and the suffragettes would carry on the fight with more fury than ever. Her death would not even remove the leader of the organisation, because Christabel safely in Paris was now planning the struggle.

A martyr for the cause

In June 1913 Emily Davison went to the Derby at Epsom, and threw herself in front of a group of horses by Tattenham Corner. She could not have picked out which horse to run in front of, though it happened to be King George

Left: *Martyrdom snowballs.* **Top:** *Arrest and demonstrations.* **Bottom:** *Emily Davison's death at the Epsom Derby, 1913. 'The Cause has need of a tragedy,' she said on one occasion*

V's horse Anmer. The jockey was thrown, but recovered; Emily Davison died of her injuries four days later.

To bring her body back from Epsom to the Davison family grave in the north of England, the coffin had to be taken from Victoria to King's Cross. This was one of the largest of all the processions for votes for women; there were supporters of the cause in black or purple or white, groups of women arranged by profession, and embroidered banners, all reminiscent of the days of peaceful demonstrations half-a-dozen years earlier. It was primarily a WSPU procession – Mrs Pankhurst was not there, for she was rearrested as soon as she stepped out of her house to take part, but women who had no sympathy with the campaign of violence could respect Emily Davison's death and find for a short time the unity and agreement that had been lost under the stress of militancy.

It was a brief respite; the WSPU soon returned to the attack. It was still dominated by the centralising tendencies of Mrs Pankhurst and Christabel; at the end of 1913 they told Sylvia to stop her activity in the East End of London, and return to the main stream of suffragette agitation. Sylvia's East End movement was becoming increasingly socialist in tendency. Christabel and Mrs Pankhurst may have felt that it was difficult enough to run a militant campaign for votes for women without going in for socialism as well, but pretty certainly jealousy and snobbery also entered into it: Sylvia was building up support among working-class women that was devoted to her rather than to the other two Pankhursts, and the other two were meeting such a lot of smart women in the cause of the struggle that they felt Sylvia was lowering the social standing of the family by going off and living in the slums.

Sylvia was not noticeably more peaceloving or accommodating than the rest of the family. She refused to give up her work, and the other two expelled her from the WSPU. But she continued with her own organisation – it ran on a smaller scale than the WSPU, because Sylvia had to combine the roles undertaken by her mother and her elder sister in the larger organisation. She worked out the plans, but she was also the martyr for the cause, constantly being arrested, going on hunger-strike, being released, and returning to the struggle. She was carried round on a stretcher, almost always with a large group of her East End housewives accompanying her and this bodyguard helped her to escape rearrest on a number of occasions.

By the beginning of 1914 suffragette tactics were becoming increasingly frantic. They went on setting fire

Right: Suffragette marchers mobbed and beaten in Wales, 1912

90

to houses, and they took to attacking pictures: the Rokeby Venus in the National Gallery was slashed, and so were a number of other less valuable paintings. The suffragette policy was to do anything as long as it was not a threat to human life—of course, if they had kept up the policy of arson, sometimes by using home-made time-bombs, sooner or later someone would have been killed and this would probably have led to a public reaction against the movement.

Lesbian undertones

Although the public resented arson and destruction, it also resented the methods used by the police. The suffragettes who were arrested and put on trial did not lack public sympathy; the demonstrations were accepted as a sign that some women were in deadly earnest. The morale and unity of the suffragettes were high: some historians, notably George Dangerfield in his *Strange Death of Liberal England,* have suggested that there was a strong tinge of lesbianism about the more militant suffragettes, but this is greatly exaggerated. Undoubtedly Christabel herself was not interested in men—though she was not as suspicious of them and their motives as the respected Susan Anthony in the United States—and it was perfectly true that many of the young militants were passionately devoted to her as their leader. In a period before Freudian analysis had made people self-conscious about their relations with members of the same sex, they could express this devotion more openly than people could do at the present day without wondering about the sexual implications of what they were saying.

Probably several active and determined girls of lesbian inclinations would join the suffragettes, but there is no real sign that they were an important part of the movement. Habits of dress provide some misleading evidence. Despite the passing of the crinoline, fashionable women's clothes had not become any less restricting and repressive, and changes in fashions in the decade before 1914 did nothing to make life easier.

Any woman who wanted to establish her position of equality with men at that time would tend to wear severe and mannish clothes; at the present day such clothes may indicate a lack of interest in men, but in the years before the First World War many women wore these clothes simply to show that they were serious-minded enough to qualify for a job. Women's fashions of the time were clearly not practical for earning a living; if a woman was going to earn her living she almost inevitably adopted a costume closely resembling that of the men among whom she worked, with, of course, the exception that she would wear a fairly long skirt.

Dangerfield supports his view about lesbianism by referring to the enthusiasm of some of Christabel's Parisian friends for the poems of Sappho. These people were not active suffragettes, and, in addition, Sappho was and is accepted as the greatest of all women poets. Any woman who was committed whole-heartedly to the cause was bound to have a great admiration for the Greek poet: almost all her writing consisted of very unrestrained love-poems to the women who lived with her, but probably this was much less important for the suffragettes than the fact that she was a woman writer who had triumphed over the handicaps placed on her sex and had become a great artist.

The type of solidarity felt by the militants was expressed by Annie Kenney, who wrote, 'No companionship can ever surpass the companionship of the militants,' and by Rachel Ferguson who wrote, 'The suffrage campaign was our Eton and Oxford, our regiment, our ship.' These comparisons made very good sense: there had not been many opportunities for women to work together, and the emotional climate of the suffragette campaign was raised by this sense that they were doing something new. Undoubtedly a good many of the hard core of determined militants found the years of conflict before 1914 the most exciting period of their lives. The youngest of the suffragettes are now in their seventies, but for most of them the time of struggle is still a happier memory than almost anything else in their lives.

This emotional satisfaction — sexual or lesbian only in a very remote sense — was very real to the suffragettes, but it could hardly affect the policy of the British government. In the years of extreme militancy the House of Commons voted on women's suffrage more seriously than before; Private Members' bills were introduced in each session. They were defeated by fairly slender margins, and a good many opponents of the bills were simply waiting for the government to take a position. A bill to extend the franchise was likely to be introduced to take the place of the one laid aside in the 1913 fiasco; many supporters of the government waited to see what form this bill would take before doing anything to help votes for women forward.

In June 1914 Asquith agreed to see a suffragette delegation. Not a WSPU delegation but a group from Sylvia

Top left: The Daily Herald *points the fresh turn of events:* 'The New Advocate' *(left) refers to Emily Davison's death;* 'Why don't they forcibly feed us?' — *a comment from a slum child (right).* **Bottom left:** *Emmeline and Sylvia Pankhurst in prison. In one year Sylvia withstood ten successive hunger-and-thirst strikes: she was fed by stomach tube twice a day*

Pankhurst's East London Federation for Women's Suffrage. Poor women, who had to look after a family and at the same time earn a little money to help the husband's wages go further, came into Downing Street to see the Prime Minister. They explained what Parliament could do for the problems of poor working women, and they made a considerable impression on Asquith.

Previously he had felt that the suffragettes were a lot of rich women making a fuss because they wanted something to do – also he had, not surprisingly, been very upset when a group of them tried to tear his clothes off when they ambushed him during a visit to Scotland. As a party leader it was his business to wonder what the electoral implications of the change would be; the more he saw of the WSPU and its steady tendency to climb up the social scale, the more he must have felt that votes for women meant votes for the Conservative Party.

But the women of the East End on the delegation were not of this sort. In straightforward electoral terms, they were likely to vote Liberal (or to turn to the infant Labour Party). In social terms they had a case; the government could do something about some of the handicaps under which they suffered; if they had the vote, they would be less likely to be overlooked. Asquith did not commit himself completely, but he went a long way towards saying that the government would bring in a bill to give votes to everyone, men and women.

The WSPU were not in the least pleased by this. Quite apart from their understandable feeling that things had gone wrong once in 1913 and might go wrong again, what Asquith had suggested was a bill for men and women, and they wanted one for women alone. So the suffragette attacks went on for another six weeks. The whole scene was transformed in August by the outbreak of the First World War; the women's organisations plunged into the war effort, with the WSPU leaders most prominent in patriotic activity and most ready to forget about the struggle to get the vote.

Right: Mrs Pankhurst is arrested outside Buckingham Palace. At her trial she said: 'I look upon myself as a prisoner of war'
Next page: A British programme advertises a demonstration against women's suffrage (left), while (right) a suffragist poster draws some damning electoral parallels. Women's suffrage remained a burning issue until the First World War closed the ranks. Ironically the first female MP to sit in the House of Commons was to be the American-born Nancy, Viscountess Astor, in 1919: ironically, because, far from being an agitator, she was actually surprised to find herself 'the first parliamentary shot to be fired by the great cannon of the women's movement'

ROYAL·ALBERT·HALL

NATIONAL LEAGUE FOR OPPOSING WOMEN'S SUFFRAGE

Demonstration

AGAINST

WOMAN SUFFRAGE

Under the

auspices of the

NATIONAL

LEAGUE

for

OPPOSING

WOMAN SUFFRAGE.

28th February,

1912,

AT 8 O'CLOCK IN

THE EVENING.

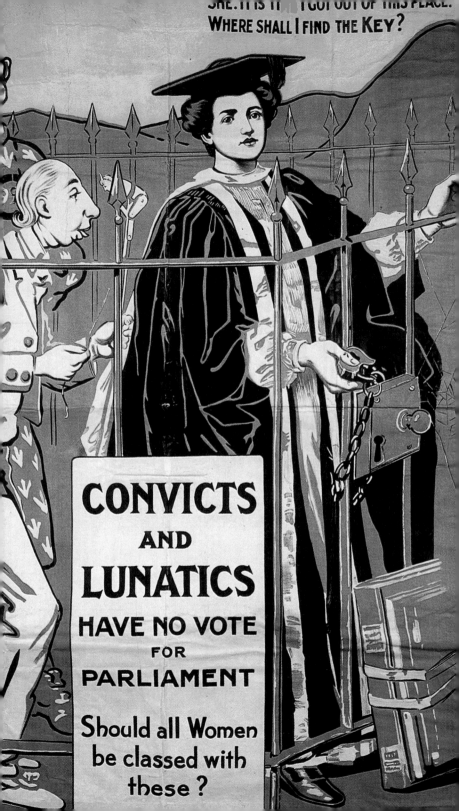

Chapter 8
The Great War

At the end of the war, when women were enfranchised (along with men) in the 1918 Representation of the People Act, it suited a lot of people to talk as if women had been given the vote simply because of what happened during the war. This does not seem very plausible; the emotional stress in England in the years just before the war was much higher than it was anywhere else during the whole long history of women's struggle to get the vote, but the women in England had been part of a movement that was gaining ground all over the world before the war — in many places inspired by the struggle in England and the Pankhurst example of leadership and self-sacrifice, which may have looked even nobler seen from afar.

The initial effect of the war was probably to delay the coming of votes for women in a few places — Asquith's response to the East London Federation suggests that English women would have got the vote in 1915. But while the war was on, there was not much change: Denmark (which at that time included Iceland) gave votes to women in 1915, and the Netherlands did so in 1917. In 1917 some women in Canada were given the vote, by an unpleasant device considered by a number of countries after the war.

The suffrage movement had not been strong in Canada before the war. Despite attempts by groups with British and groups with American connections, there was not much response. Canada was not highly urbanised, and the large Catholic section in Quebec was traditionally-minded and showed every sign of resenting the 20th century. To the normal Catholic feelings in favour of women remaining devoted to family life, there was added the political calculation that if they raised large families the Catholics of Quebec might become numerically dominant in the electorate — ('la revanche des berceaux' or 're-venge through the cradle').

Canada entered the war without doubts or misgivings, but it was soon clear that English-speaking Canada was

Left: Workroom of a British war hospital supply depot, First World War. Girls of genteel background could now feel useful

far more whole-heartedly committed to it than French-speaking Canada. The demand for manpower became so intense that Canadian units could not be kept up to strength without conscription, but by this time Quebec was no longer ready to co-operate. Most of the Liberals from outside Quebec joined the Conservative government to impose conscription; the anti-conscription Liberals were obviously going to win almost every French-speaking seat in Quebec. The Coalition government needed to win every seat it could in English-speaking Canada, and it passed a Wartime Elections Act which, apart from measures like disenfranchising immigrants from Germany or Austria-Hungary, gave votes to women with husbands or other close relations in the forces. It could be taken for granted that they would vote for the Conservatives, simply to make sure that the war effort was maintained and their relations at the front were not deserted.

All women were given the right to vote in nation-wide elections the next year – provinces could make their own rules and while all the others had enfranchised women by 1922, Quebec waited until 1940. But the Canadian example of differential enfranchisement, based on war service, was adopted after the war by Belgium (which did not give universal suffrage until after the Second World War), and was considered in a number of other countries.

The vote and post-war regimes
When the war was over, it turned out that defeat in battle was what really helped the cause of votes for women. In Russia women got the vote in 1917 when their country was collapsing under the weight of the attack from Germany and Austria-Hungary and, whatever the other aspects of Communism may be, it has all the time been a noticeable feature of life in the Soviet Union that women are closer to equality with men than in most other countries outside Scandinavia. In Sweden, which had been neutral during the war, the parties of the left had opposed Germany, and the parties of the right had been pro-German. In November 1918 the parties of the left organised demonstrations in the streets of Stockholm, which pointed to the possibility of revolution, and to pacify them the government carried out several reforms in the next two or three years, including giving women the vote.

In 1918 Germany and Austria-Hungary themselves collapsed, and their Emperors were overthrown. Votes for women came naturally when the Weimar Republic under the Social Democrats was set up in Germany. Austria-Hungary disintegrated into the various national

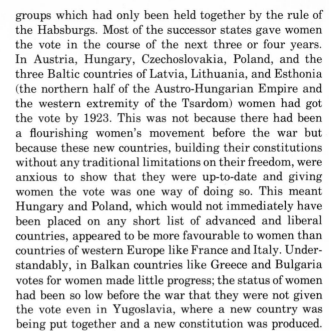

groups which had only been held together by the rule of the Habsburgs. Most of the successor states gave women the vote in the course of the next three or four years. In Austria, Hungary, Czechoslovakia, Poland, and the three Baltic countries of Latvia, Lithuania, and Esthonia (the northern half of the Austro-Hungarian Empire and the western extremity of the Tsardom) women had got the vote by 1923. This was not because there had been a flourishing women's movement before the war but because these new countries, building their constitutions without any traditional limitations on their freedom, were anxious to show that they were up-to-date and giving women the vote was one way of doing so. This meant Hungary and Poland, which would not immediately have been placed on any short list of advanced and liberal countries, appeared to be more favourable to women than countries of western Europe like France and Italy. Understandably, in Balkan countries like Greece and Bulgaria votes for women made little progress; the status of women had been so low before the war that they were not given the vote even in Yugoslavia, where a new country was being put together and a new constitution was produced.

But France and Italy showed that even in advanced countries, if there was no violent shock to the political system, women would not get the right to vote unless they organised a powerful body of opinion. Roman Catholic influence could hardly be blamed for the resistance; in 1919 Pope Benedict XV commended the cause of votes for women. The question was discussed in both countries just after the war; it was passed by the French Chamber of Deputies in 1919, but the Radical party's fear that women voters would be influenced by the Church meant that the women's cause lost the support of some people who might have been expected to be on its side. The measure was delayed, and eventually was rejected in 1922 by the Senate for the first but by no means the last time. In 1936 Blum's Popular Front government appointed three women under-secretaries in the ministry, although they did not have the vote and could not sit in the Chamber, but liberalisation got no further before 1939.

In Italy the question was discussed in the first few years after the war, but Mussolini's seizure of power in 1922 ended any prospect of an improvement in the position of women. The rise of Fascism and Nazism was a setback to the women's cause all over Europe — ingenious male political theorists might argue that Communism and Fascism were just the same thing but the Communist

Left: German comments on the way in which the war created new jobs for women, and so prepared men for post-war changes

101

countries did bring equality for women, and the Fascist rulers believed in Church, children and the kitchen for women *(Kirche, kinder und küche)*.

Women's war work

The two real triumphs for agitation were in England and the United States. To be sure, women did play an important part in the war in both countries, but then they played an important part in the war in almost all the countries concerned. For the first time a war was being fought in which nations could bring out their whole capacity for working and fighting. The efforts of English women have been studied more than any others, because the English were anxious to show that it was by war service that women had earned the right to vote, and other countries were not so concerned about this side of the case.

If the work of English women can be covered in detail, it must not be forgotten that in other countries women were taking up new types of work; in France this was not so easy, because a great deal of the new work undertaken by women was to replace men in the factories where armaments and explosives were produced. So many French factories were in the part of France that had been overrun by the first wave of the German advance in 1914 that French women did not have so much opportunity to take on new jobs. In Germany the jobs were more available, and of course it was in Germany that women suffered most during the war – except in the sense that all women suffered from the deaths of men at the front – because Germany was in the grip of a tight blockade imposed by the Royal Navy and the German government was not good at planning how to deal with the domestic effects of the blockade. Substitutes were provided for explosives and for metals that used to be imported, but the food supply deteriorated, everybody was underfed and most people were hungry. In the absence of an effective rationing system, women spent their time queuing for what there was to buy.

Quite apart from the English desire to show how much women had done in the war, the situation changed much more in England than in any other European country during the war. The other countries had conscript armies, and knew that when war broke out most of the young men of fighting age would go away and would have to be replaced. No such arrangements had been made in England; millions of volunteers responded to the great poster of

Top left: English women at war work. Queen Mary entered in her wartime diary: 'Worked from 3 to 5 planting potatoes. Got very hot and tired.' ***Bottom left:*** *Tramway girls in Milan*

Kitchener pointing a warning finger and saying 'Your Country Needs You', but nobody had thought very much what would happen next. Even when conscription became necessary, people had not really worked out what to do.

For the first twelve months or so, the position of women in England was more or less unchanged by the war. The slogan 'business as usual' was launched by *The Daily Mail,* partly because women were being put out of work in the early stages of the war. Servants were being paid off, dress-making and the other demands of the social season provided much less work than usual, and at first there seemed to be no other jobs to do. But steadily the effects of the surge of volunteers into the army began to be felt, and so did the increasing demands for munitions. More shells were needed to blast a path through the German lines. Women who had been out of work now found it fairly easy to get jobs, often under better conditions than ever before. People admired the women who went off to work in shell factories, pouring liquid TNT into the canisters, running the risk of being blown up or—less drastic but still unpleasant—being stained bright yellow by picric acid. No doubt some of the munitions workers were making a sacrifice for the war effort; however, many of them had been doing more uncomfortable jobs for equally long hours, at lower wages and with much less security of employment, in the years before the war.

Women who had never previously worked did not often go into factory jobs, though some of them set up canteens in the factories as part of the war-time tendency to improve working conditions. But many more nurses were needed than before, and many of the new recruits were women from the comfortable classes who felt that they were now doing something useful; it was an unfortunate side-effect that their willingness to work for low wages encouraged everybody to think nursing was a vocation for which a living wage was quite unnecessary.

The woman whose fate attracted more attention than any other during the war was Nurse Cavell. She stayed on in Brussels when the German invasion overran Belgium. She and her nurses looked after wounded soldiers of all nationalities, but she also helped English and French soldiers to escape, usually to Holland where they were interned and could not return to fight. Helping soldiers escape was a violation of the rules evolved in order to give nurses some official position and immunity in battle, and no doubt she deserved some sort of punishment. But the Germans shot her—unchivalrous and inhumane, and unwise as well. She did indeed say 'Patriotism is not enough' but she also said 'I am glad to die for my country' and the execution certainly helped the

104

Index Numbers of Female Employment in France, 1914-18

(July 1914 = 100)

1 Chemical Industries
2 Timber & Carpentry
3 Metal Industries
4 Construction & Quarries
5 Administration & Transp

portion of Female to
le Employment
he UK, 1914-20

ndustry
ransport
overnment Establishments
griculture
inance & Commerce
ocal Government
otal of all employment

1914
2%
3%
9%
27%
34%
24%

1918
12%
14%
47%
53%
52%
37%

1920
4%
5%
10%
40%
36%
28%

British war effort. The Germans had been accused of atrocities in Belgium, but nothing was easy to prove because the Germans were in control in Belgium. Now the Germans had shot a nurse in Belgium many of the other stories looked more probable.

As the war went on it became more and more necessary to take a rational attitude to the supply of manpower, and very often this meant getting women who could take on work done by men. Women continued to take on office jobs, at a time when there was more and more office work to be done, keeping up with the forms and official documents which are an inevitable part of modern war. There were women bus conductors – cartoonists and photographers made a great fuss about them, though in fact there had been a few before the war. Women had always worked on farms; now 'land girls' from the towns volunteered to help on farms for the war effort and they were a great deal more use than the pessimistic farmers had thought they would be. England was never as short of food as Germany in the war, but the risk of submarine blockade was there, and more food had to be grown.

And women went closer to the battle than this. The women's auxiliary services – quite distinct from nursing – provided a range of services from lorry-driving to running field-telephone systems. The war showed that women could do almost all the jobs that men did. Before the war they had been slowly moving forward into almost every sort of work, but nobody noticed it or wondered what happened next. The war, when women at work suddenly became a vital part of the nation's efforts, showed men that life had changed, and made them ready to do a certain amount to accept the change.

Success at last
The idea of enfranchising all adult males, which the Liberals had been considering without too much enthusiasm in the years before the war, now became something that obviously had to be passed into law. And it was almost equally obvious that votes for women had to come as well. The suffragettes had laid down their stones and their matches and their chains as soon as war was declared – several of them equipped themselves with white feathers instead, which they thrust with indiscriminate fervour at men not in uniform, sometimes insulting men back from the trenches and making skilled munitions workers give up their factory jobs (in which they were hard to replace) to go off and fight. The militant spirit had not disappeared; it had just found new

Left: Diagrams illustrating the influx of women into men's jobs in the United Kingdom and France in the First World War

channels through which to flow. If votes for women had been refused, the spirit of the suffragettes could quite easily have arisen again.

The committee, under the chairmanship of the Speaker of the House of Commons, which worked out the principles for the 1918 Act, saw that there were more women than men in the population – mainly because of the pattern of births, partly because of losses in war. The men were alarmed by the idea of a female majority in the electorate; facing a comparable situation fifty years previously Gladstone had argued for an expansion of the electorate by saying 'they are our own flesh and blood', but the Speaker's Conference was more suspicious. It suggested that all men should be given the vote at twenty-one, and that women should get the vote at thirty.

Many of the leaders in the struggle for the vote did stand in the 1918 election, but none of them were successful – most of them stood as Labour or Liberal candidates in opposition to Lloyd George's Liberal-Conservative coalition government. Christabel Pankhurst was given a fair, but not a good, chance: she contested Smethwick, as a Coalition candidate with the support of Lloyd George. She was defeated by the Labour Party candidate though she polled more votes than any other woman standing.

One woman was elected in 1918, though for reasons which had nothing to do with votes for women. Countess Markievicz (born Constance Gore-Booth, sister of Eva Gore-Booth, who had helped set Mrs Pankhurst on the road to revolutionary action) was an Irish nationalist, who had come quite close to being executed for her share in the Easter Rising in Dublin in 1916. In 1918 she was elected as the *Sinn Fein* candidate for South Dublin. Like the other *Sinn Fein* MPs, she did not go to Westminster but took her place in the *Dail* which declared itself to be the legal government of Ireland. When the Irish Free State had won its independence, it allowed women to vote at the same age as men. The age discrimination remained in force in England until another act was passed in 1928, though by that time all the excitement had gone out of the fight.

This was a silly little tailpiece to the struggle for the vote in England, caused by the foolish belief that all the women were going to vote for women candidates and swamp the men. Women are a majority of the electorate in a good many countries, but nowhere do they have anything like a majority of the seats in Parliament, Congress, or representative assembly. Several new classes of people have won the right to vote during the last hundred and fifty years, but very few of these new classes

Left: Contrasts of peacetime and wartime industry in France

have followed up their success by going into politics. Negroes make up almost a tenth of the electorate in the United States, but have nothing like a tenth of the seats in Congress; the manual working class make up between a half and two-thirds of the electorate in England, but have nothing like half the seats in the House of Commons. And women, who were an excluded class in just the same way as the Negroes and manual workers, are no more likely to end up with as many parliamentary seats as their numbers in the population would suggest.

America plays for time
The last important stage of the struggle for votes for women came in the United States. In the Congress elected in 1916 there was a clear majority for votes for women — obviously any Senator or Representative who came from the state which had given women the vote was going to support votes for women whenever it came up. This gave women a form of pressure on Congress which was more useful than the election of a woman Representative — Jeanette Rankin from Wyoming was elected for the first time in 1916, and she did show people that a Congresswoman was not an impossibility.

However, in the restricted undercover struggle in Congress she was probably a bit of a handicap for the supporters of votes for women. Her strong pacifist convictions made her vote against the decision that the United States should join the war against Germany in 1917, and this was not popular. It was used by some opponents of votes for women to suggest that the suffragettes were unpatriotic; the NAWSA had laid down that its members could take whatever side they chose about the war, but the accusation had some effect. Besides this, she had to take an important role in the suffrage debates because she was the only woman in Congress, but because she was new to the job she did not know all the pitfalls that had to be avoided. The enemies of votes for women relied on fear of the unknown to hold their votes united, and the task inside Congress was to soothe them and show at least some of the opponents that their fears were unjustified. Jeanette Rankin had not had enough practice at the job to know how to go about soothing the doubters.

A clear majority was not enough. The NAWSA had accepted the policy of the Susan Anthony amendment (and the policy of the Women's Party, though they would never say so) of getting Congress to present a consti-

Left: Not only did the war create opportunities for women, it also caused scarcities on the home front, as 'The Food Queue', a pastel by C.R.W. Nevinson, illustrates. In both ways attention was drawn to the needs and grievances of women

109

tutional amendment to the forty-eight states. If Congress accepted an amendment to the constitution by a two-thirds majority, then the states would have to hold special meetings of the legislatures to discuss the amendment. In these special meetings opponents would not be able to use procedural devices to stop the subject being discussed; they would have to come to a vote and declare themselves. All sorts of people who thought votes for women were undesirable would not care to say so in public – in particular, politicians would be afraid to vote against it, if they thought women were soon going to get the vote. Naturally, the more hostile to women a politician was, the more likely he was to think that they would be vindictive once they had got the vote and would throw out everybody who had been seen to vote against their cause.

So, once the amendment was through Congress, it would probably not have much more trouble, outside the South. The difficulty was to get Congress, and in particular the Senate, to do anything. At the beginning of 1918 the House of Representatives voted for the amendment by 274 votes to 136 – a two-thirds majority, but the very barest two-thirds majority, and it is fairly certain that some Congressmen did not vote against the amendment but hoped that the Senate could do something to stop it. The House of Representatives is not easy to stir into action, but at least it does have ways of getting a vote if a clear majority wants one. The Senate has even more ways of avoiding a vote, and only a two-thirds majority can force one.

So the opponents of votes for women conducted a delaying action. This was a bit of a gamble. State after state was changing its own constitution and enfranchising women, and each such change meant that the Senators from the state became committed to votes for women unless they had made up their minds to retire from politics. Besides, American women were playing their part in the mounting war effort, and this provided fresh arguments for the supporters of change. There was nothing like the Second World War 'Rosie the Riveter' to suggest that women could do any job a man had done before the war, but women were needed as nurses, and as the United States committed itself to providing a vast modern army a great many men were summoned from their work and their jobs had to be filled.

No doubt some of the people who changed their minds and said that women ought to have the vote because they were doing so much in the war were just looking for a polite excuse to switch from one side of the fence to the other. Still, some men had simply not realised how much the world had changed in the previous fifty years; if the

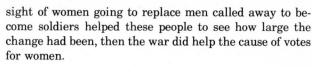

sight of women going to replace men called away to become soldiers helped these people to see how large the change had been, then the war did help the cause of votes for women.

The final stages in America

The activities of the Women's Party at this stage pretty certainly handicapped the cause. All through 1918 supporters of the change tried to get a few extra votes in the Senate and at the same time tried to get the Senate to come to a vote. The backbone of the Senate came from the South—courteous and determined old gentlemen who were afraid of the future but not unwilling to be reassured about it. President Wilson tried persuading a few of the more malleable Senators to see things his way; he could appeal to them as fellow-Democrats and point out that, while they might be safe for re-election, the party needed to show it was friendly to women to secure its position in Congress and to elect a Democratic President.

The Women's Party continued to apply the methods of the English suffragettes at a time when they were quite out of place: women chaining themselves to railings and screaming were exactly what the Southern Senators were afraid of. The Women's Party thought it would be fun to burn Wilson in effigy; in fact the police stoppped them making fools of themselves, but it was not at all clear what burning him was meant to do. Of course, if he had had the power to get the amendment passed and had been holding it up—in short, if he had been in the position of Asquith five years previously—it would have been understandable that the suffragettes were cross with him. But Wilson did not have the powers of the English Prime Minister (as he had pointed out with more than a hint of regret in his books on the American constitution) and he was doing the best he could for votes for women.

Eventually, in the last few weeks of the Congress elected in 1916, the Senate came to a vote, and the constitutional amendment was not able to get the two-thirds majority it needed. But in the new Congress, which had already been elected, there was a large majority for the amendment in the House of Representatives, and the opponents felt more ready than ever to leave the work of resistance to the Senate. But in the Senate a spirit of caution was at work. Not many people changed their minds, but a dozen or so Senators stayed away. Those who stayed away but were really opposed to votes for women were of course making it easier for the amendment to get a two-thirds majority, which it did in June 1919.

*Left: The New Womanhood of France and Germany flexes its muscles: **(top)** at sport, **(bottom)** in the coal and shoe industries*

LA NATATION

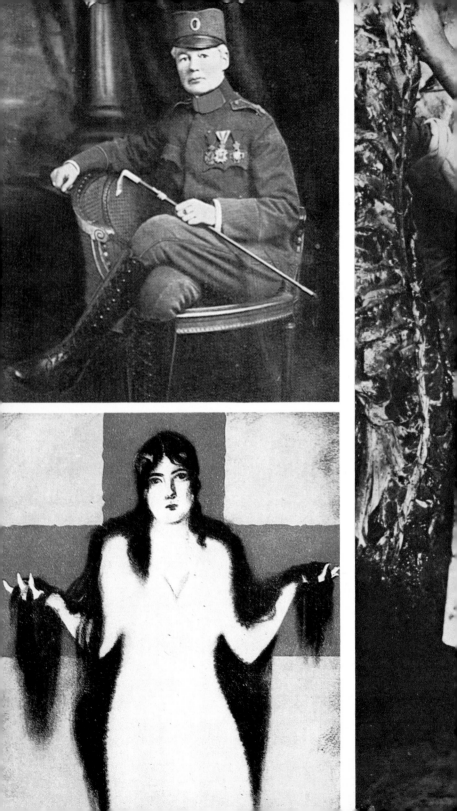

The last stage, getting the state legislatures to confirm the amendment, took another fourteen months. Most of it went easily and smoothly, but the opposition still had some hope in New England and the South. By March 1920 the struggle had, appropriately enough, come down to a border state: Tennessee seemed the best immediate hope of finding a thirty-sixth state and passing the Susan Anthony amendment to the constitution. But the Governor of the State had no desire to see the matter discussed; he knew that the losers were going to be bitter after the fight, and he was not so sure that the victors – whichever side they were – would be grateful. The result of his delay was that the legislature did not meet until August, the hottest month of the year, when temperatures would make every man and woman wilt.

A vast band of lobbyists descended on Nashville to encourage the legislators to see things their way. Prohibition and the Volstead Act, which defined intoxicating liquors as beverages containing 'one half of one per centum or more of alcohol by volume', were already in effect, but nobody took the slightest notice. The NAWSA lobbyists claimed to be surprised at the sight of legislators going round drunk; in fact they probably knew what would happen, but thought it would be useful to tell everyone else what nasty people the opponents of votes for women really were. The supporters of votes for women reckoned they had the votes, and they also had the backing of the federal party organisations, neither of which wanted to look less enthusiastic about votes for women than the others. So the supporters of the constitutional amendment wanted the Tennessee legislature to keep cool hands and vote quickly; the opponents wanted to delay things, and the more muddled and fuddled they could get the legislature the better for their side.

But after a couple of weeks of this the legislators wanted to go home; and they passed the Susan Anthony amendment by 49 votes to 47. The NAWSA leaders went to Washington to see the signing of the official Proclamation of the Amendment. They were too late; the official responsible for the Proclamation had not wanted any further delay and as soon as he heard that Tennessee had voted he issued the document, without waiting for the victorious women's leaders.

Top left: Sergeant-Major Flora Sandes, 'the only British woman in the Serbian army'. *Bottom left:* German poster asks women to save their hair—for the war effort. *Left:* Berlin's first female butcher: anything a man could do, a woman could do too

Epilogue

And so the struggle was over. In the next twenty years about a dozen countries gave women the vote — most of them Latin American countries where the vote was often frustrated by military revolutions. The vote recognised women's equality, but really it came too late to help do much about it. If women had had the vote in the 19th century, they could have used it to help themselves forward in many struggles for economic advance and for the right to enter professions; as it was, they had to fight their way forward without the help of the vote, and in fact were able to do so with considerable success. In a way, the vote came after the battle had been won, though the struggle for the vote was one way for women to remind men — and to remind themselves — that they were not being given an equal chance. Efforts to stop women getting the vote were an attempt to pretend that nothing had changed in the 19th century and that women were still willing to live at home or to be overworked and underpaid.

If votes for women, by the time they were granted, were a monument to past progress, another event in 1918 — the publication of Marie Stopes's *Married Love* — was a pointer to the future. By present-day standards it is a very mild and unexciting book (only by an effort of historical imagination can one see why the British Museum had special arrangements for people who wanted to read it). But when it came out it was sensational: the witty and sophisticated Lady Diana Manners, who had been the leader of a little group that called itself the 'corrupt coterie', found it immensely worthwhile, and recommended it to her friends; the book had enormous sales and ran into legal problems on the grounds that it was outspoken on subjects that ought not to be discussed.

The book gave a simple account of intercourse and of contraceptive methods, presented Dr Stopes's theory of

Left: *Japanese factory women hold a meeting to demonstrate against starvation wages. The ability to earn an independent living was in urban countries almost a precondition of suffrage*

the times at which a woman would be most enthusiastic about sex, and stressed the fact that it was the husband's duty to make sure that his wife was in a receptive frame of mind. The success of the book does suggest that a good many married couples were still in the state indicated by the legendary mother's advice to the young bride: 'Lie still and think of England.'

Acceptance of the fact that women could expect something more than this in marriage, and acceptance of the fact that women do not necessarily have to get married first, have been among the larger changes in the position of women in the last fifty years. But there have been a great many others; equality in sexual matters has been among the most-widely discussed, but it rests on equality, or at least on greater opportunity, in a whole lot of other areas of life. 'Man must work from dawn till set of sun, but woman's work is never done' had some grim truth when sewing was done by hand, sweeping and brushing was done by hand, and when all rooms were heated (if at all) by coal fires and almost all meals were cooked by coal fires.

Middle-class comforts

Changes in these respects were coming in the years just before 1914 – Margot Asquith installed a bathroom in 10 Downing Street, which does not mean that Asquith was the first clean Prime Minister, but simply that water had previously been carried to the bedrooms by the servants and then carried down again. Gas and electricity for heating and for cooking, electricity for sewing-machines and vacuum cleaners, meant that women had less work to do, and what had to be done took less physical effort. These changes were beginning to affect middle-class homes at just about the time that the struggle for the vote was getting going: it was after women had got the vote that these benefits began to spread down to the working-class.

Possibly if women had had to choose between electricity and the vote, they would have been wise to choose electricity, though of course the choice never came in those terms. Once the vote had been won, it served mainly as a defensive weapon; politicians, and men in general, knew that there were some things they could no longer get away with, though on questions like equal pay for equal work they could hold their position for many years to come. Although they might not be going to do anything positive with their votes, women valued them for their defensive power, and took it for granted that the vote was worth having.

The story of the struggle for the vote almost inevitably concentrates on developments in the rich and advanced

116

nations. For example, the existence of office-jobs which gave women a fair chance of earning their own living at a middle-class level in big cities was an important factor in the spread of the suffrage movement. These jobs hardly existed outside the North Atlantic area and Australia and New Zealand. Outside these fortunate areas the right to vote was often denied to men as well as women; even in areas like Latin America, which theoretically believed in the right to vote, the harsh reality of the military *coup d'état* was almost as common a way of bringing about a change of government. When men did not care so much about the right to vote women were not going to press the point.

Progress in traditional societies

In the less prosperous nations, rich women were locked up, poor women were beasts of burden and there was no middle class to speak of. The ways in which rich women were locked up varied from continent to continent. In Latin America the influence of the Church, the duenna system, and a strict application of a double standard of sexual morality for men and for women combined to keep rich women strictly confined to private life. The harem system in Moslem countries, purdah in India, and the complex Chinese ceremonies of which foot-binding (wrapping up ladies' feet in tight bandages so that they remained delicately small, at the cost of crippling the women) is the best known, all had the same effect.

Of course, only the rich could go in for these elaborate performances. The women of the poor had to work, and wore themselves out in work and constant child-bearing just as in the more prosperous countries. The difference was the absence of any large class between the rich and the poor.

For a good many years the women's best hope of progress in these countries was that men were anxious to imitate the customs of the prosperous and dominant North Atlantic countries. People who wanted to be up-to-date all saw it in terms of following the pattern set in the West, and votes for women was part of the pattern.

Other customs had to change: respectable women had worn the veil in almost all Moslem countries, as a sign that they were cut off from the world outside their homes. Reformers like Atatürk in Turkey and Zaghlul in Egypt opposed the veil as one symptom of the backwardness of their countries—when Egyptian women showed that they had taken one step towards emancipation by coming out into the streets of Cairo in 1919 to demonstrate against

Left: *Indian suffragettes, 1911. Women's suffrage was often a by-product of successful anti-colonial nationalist movements*

117

British rule, Zaghlul reminded them of another aspect of emancipation by tearing the veil off one of the demonstrators.

For politicians living under colonial rule and trying to reduce its power, 'freedom' was naturally the leading slogan. Freedom from colonial rule for men, and also a bit of freedom for women. In English colonies women's political equality was recognised after 1918 and when men got the right to vote women also received it, usually on the same terms. In India, Burma, and Ceylon women got the vote as a natural result of the national movement towards independence.

In the independent country of Turkey women got the vote (fairly certainly to the disgust of the majority of male and female voters) because Atatürk saw this as part of his struggle to bring his country into the modern world. Of course, a small group of women appreciated the change; the sort of women who went to International Women's Suffrage Association meetings were glad that progress had been made, but obviously they were a tiny minority who could not have brought about the change by their own efforts. Even if they had been as determined as the suffragettes in England it would have done them little good; the militant suffragettes depended on the support of a large body of sympathisers, and the progressive women of Turkey (and a great many similar countries) would have found very little support among their countrywomen.

In a few Latin American countries women got the right to vote around 1930. Countries like Brazil, Cuba, Uruguay, and Ecuador were reasonably prosperous, and were willing to imitate the United States by giving votes to women. There was something rather haphazard about the process: in Mexico and Argentina the vote spread slowly on a province-by-province basis and in Chile, which was as developed as any of the others, women acquired the right to vote only in municipal elections.

By the late 1930s women had the vote pretty well all over the world, and it was seen as an inevitable development, though people were taking their time over doing anything about the inevitable.

Since the war

The Second World War, another war for democracy, established the point beyond all argument. Almost every European country was shattered by the war and had to start all over again by establishing a new constitution, and nearly all of them gave votes to women. An exception still remained: Switzerland had not been shaken by either war, and remains unshaken to this day. Swiss women are independent and are rather well-paid but still they have

118

Female Office Workers in Great Britain 1901-1961
(figures in thousands)

1385
638
527
179
89

'01 '11 '21 '31 '51

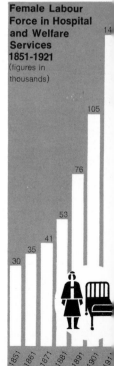

Female Labour Force in Hospital and Welfare Services 1851-1921
(figures in thousands)

14
105
76
53
41
35
30

'51 '61 '71 '81 '91 '01 '11

**ale Labour Force
e Clothing Industry
-1921**
s in thousands)

96 594 667 759 792 825 602

661 1871 1881 1891 1901 1911 1921

**ale Labour Force
e Textile
ustry
-1921**
es in
ands)

76 726 745 795 870 701

661 1871 1881 1891 1901 1911 1921

the vote in only a few cantons. They have made a little progress in the 1960s but in some ways the vote has not seemed very relevant; nobody would say that Swiss women are noticeably less free than French women or Italian women, both of whom got the vote in the aftermath of the Second World War. Scandinavian women are more free than any of them, but this is because of the cultural background and attitude to life of people in the Scandinavian countries rather than because women there have had the vote for a long time. Women in Australia have had the vote longer than women in Scandinavian countries, but they are probably less likely to be treated as equals by men than women in England or the United States. On the American frontier women were expected to do the same sort of work as men and keep the light of civilisation burning as well, but in the frontier conditions of Australia women had no real place. The Australian idea of mateship was for men only, and votes for women was the triumph of political ideals that did not correspond with men's real social attitudes. No criticism meant of Australia: the Australian example cheered and inspired many people to work for votes for women when the cause looked far from hopeful in the rest of the world. But if the equality that women wanted was something more than political, the vote was not an effective way of getting it (though nobody has found a better).

Women politicians of today

None of the women who took a leading part in the struggle went on to have distinguished political careers. Christabel Pankhurst never got into the Commons, and after a while she (like Victoria Woodhull and Annie Besant before her) took up a spiritualist form of religion. Jeanette Rankin was defeated for Congress on account of her vote against going into the First World War, and did not return to Congress until the 1940 election. Her pacifist ideals, held as firmly as ever, led her to vote against going into the Second World War, with the same result. At the age of eighty-eight she has taken part in protests against United States policy in Vietnam.

More recently several women have managed to go into politics with greater success. One woman Cabinet Minister seems to be about the quota in most of the countries where they play any noticeable role in politics, though American Cabinets (which are fairly small) usually contain no women and in England there have recently been two women together in the Cabinet. Ceylon was the first country to have a woman Prime Minister,

Left: Diagrams illustrating the pattern of female labour in Britain, where economic indispensability was crucial to the vote

119

when Mrs Bandaranaike was elected; it is fair to say that she had originally been chosen as leader of her party as a tribute to her husband after his assassination. In India there is a woman Prime Minister: Mrs Gandhi is perhaps the best person that could have been found for the job and it is no disrespect to her (it is more of a criticism of the male prejudice which Indian politicians share with all other politicians) to say that she would certainly not have been chosen if her father had not been the great leader in the struggle for independence, Jawaharlal Nehru. Golda Meir, who became Prime Minister of Israel in 1969, seems to have been the first woman to become head of a government without any help from family connections.

It might be asked what women got from the struggle. Social and political advances are not directly related to the vote; political advance has been strictly limited almost everywhere to the right to choose between a couple of men. It is not just a joke at the women's expense to say that the important thing was that they managed to get their own way. The vote was the great issue on which men wanted to resist women – not all men, just as not all women wanted the vote. But enough men resisted to make it a real test case, and eventually the women proved their point: if there was something they really wanted, and really believed would make them equal with men, they could get it if they worked hard enough.

Top right: Men abandon their former positions and join the bandwagon. Top left: The final coming of age: Life magazine, October 1920. Bottom right: End of the struggle in America. San Francisco suffragettes celebrate California's ratification of the Susan Anthony amendment, November 1919

Chronology of Events

1784 The Duchess of Devonshire canvasses for Charles James Fox at the Westminster election

1825 William Thompson's *Appeal of One Half the Human Race against the Pretensions of the Other Half* advocates votes for women

1848 **July:** a women's rights meeting is held at Seneca Falls in New York State

1866 **7th June:** John Stuart Mill presents his Woman Suffrage Petition to the House of Commons

1867 The Second Reform Bill is debated and Mill moves an amendment to give votes to women. It is defeated by 194 votes to 73

1868 The National Society for Women's Suffrage is founded in England

1869 In France Léon Richier publishes *The Rights of Women*. In England, Mill's *On the Subjection of Women* is published

1871 Josephine Butler's fight against the Contagious Diseases Acts causes dissension among the women's suffrage societies

1882 The Married Women's Property Act is passed granting married women rights of separate ownership over every kind of property

1890 The National American Woman Suffrage Association is founded. Wyoming becomes a state of the Union and women are given the right to vote for Congressmen and President. During the 1890s Western Australia, South Australia, and three more western states in the USA enfranchise women

1893 The reforming Liberal-Labour government in New Zealand gives women the vote

1903 **October:** the Women's Social and Political Union is founded by Mrs Emmeline Pankhurst

1905 **13th October:** Sir Edward Grey addresses a liberal meeting in Manchester; Annie Kenney and Christabel Pankhurst are imprisoned for causing an uproar

1907 Finnish women are given the vote. In England suffragists and suffragettes hold separate marches

1908 **June:** suffrage societies hold a combined procession from the Embankment to the Albert Hall; the next weekend the WSPU holds its own open-air demonstration at Hyde Park. Emmeline and Christabel Pankhurst and Mrs Flora Drummond are imprisoned after a meeting held in Trafalgar Square

1910- 12 Six more American states give women the vote by referendum

1911 In New York the Triangle Fire arouses interest in many reforms including women's suffrage

1912 In New York suffragists parade. In England, suffragettes heckle Lloyd George at a meeting at the Royal Albert Hall

1913 In the USA Alice Paul and Lucy Burns launch the Congressional Union which becomes the American equivalent of the WSPU
March: a women's parade in Washington on President Wilson's inauguration leads to a riot when it is held up by an anti-suffrage mob
June: Emily Davison is killed when she throws herself under King George V's horse at the Derby

1915 Denmark (including Iceland) gives women the vote

1917 Women of the Netherlands and Russia get the vote

1918 In England the Representation of the People Act gives the vote to all men over twenty-one and all women over thirty

1920 Women get the vote in the United States

1922 All women in English-speaking Canada are enfranchised

1923 By this year Austria, Hungary, Czechoslovakia, Poland, Latvia, Lithuania, and Esthonia have given women the vote

1928 Women in England are given the vote at twenty-one

Top: 'Scare me, will you?': short shrift for the mouse of Man's Supremacy (left); pin-up power (middle); 'The Right Dishonourable Double-Face Asquith' (right). Centre: Keir Hardie with suffragettes (left); Rosa Luxemburg (middle); Lloyd George 'land girls' (right). Bottom: 'At Last!' — Punch cartoon, 1918 (left); Marie Stopes (middle); 'les Tommettes' (female Tommies), nickname of the British Women's Army Auxiliary Corps (right)

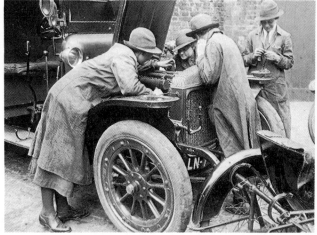

Index of main people, places and events

125

Author's suggestions for further reading

Some women's suffrage organisations produced massive histories of their work when the struggle was over; the American history is especially ponderous. However, *Woman Suffrage and Politics* by Carrie Chapman Catt and Nettie Shuler (Charles Scribner's and Sons, New York 1923) explains cross-currents much better than authors writing about other countries have done. Mildred Adams's *The Right of the People* (Lippincott, Philadelphia 1967) is a straightforward pro-suffrage history of the movement in the United States. Johanna Johnston's *Mrs Satan* (Macmillan, London 1968) is a sympathetic biography of Victoria Woodhull; Alice Blackwell's *Lucy Stone* (Little, Brown and Co., Boston 1930) may balance the picture by giving an account of a more orthodox early suffrage leader.

In England the respectable wing of the movement can be studied in Rachel Strachey's *Millicent Garrett Fawcett* (John Murray, London 1931) and *The Cause* (Kennikat, New York 1969) and the violent wing in Sylvia Pankhurst's *The Suffragette Movement* (Longmans, London 1931); both authors make an effort to see the case for the other wing (which is more than can be said for some Pankhurst books). Among more recent works two books by David Mitchell, *The Fighting Pankhursts* (Cape, London 1967) and *Women on the Warpath* (Cape 1966), give a good overall picture of the movement. Roger Fulford's *Votes for Women* (Faber 1957) tends to be facetious; Constance Rover's *Women's Suffrage and Party Politics 1866-1914* (Routledge, London 1967) is firmly partisan and ignores most of the difficulties of politics.

The subject attracts perhaps less attention outside the English-speaking world but Simone de Beauvoir's *The Second Sex* (Four Square Books 1969), one of the most famous feminist books of this century, has chapters about votes for women. Maurice Duverger's *Political Role of Women* (UNESCO, Paris 1955) surveys the way women have used the vote in various countries. A United Nations booklet, *Civic and Political Education of Women* (1964), gives the main dates of the struggle for every country in the world.

Library of the 20th Century will include the following titles:

Russia in Revolt
David Floyd
The Second Reich
Harold Kurtz
The Anarchists
Roderick Kedward
Suffragettes International
Trevor Lloyd
War by Time-Table
A.J.P.Taylor
Death of a Generation
Alistair Horne
Suicide of the Empires
Alan Clark
Twilight of the Habsburgs
Z.A.B.Zeman
Early Aviation
Sir Robert Saundby
Birth of the Movies
D.J.Wenden
Theodore Roosevelt
A.E.Campbell
Lenin's Russia
G.Katkov
The Weimar Republic
Sefton Delmer
Out of the Lion's Paw
Constantine Fitzgibbon
Japan: The Years of Triumph
Louis Allen
Communism Takes China
C.P.Fitzgerald
Black and White in South Africa
G.H.Le May
Woodrow Wilson
R.H.Ferrell
France 1918-34
W.Knapp
France 1934-40
A.N.Wahl
Mussolini's Italy
Geoffrey Warner
The Little Dictators
A.Polonsky
Viva Zapata
L.Bethell
The World Depression
Malcolm Falkus
Stalin's Russia
A.Nova
The Brutal Reich
Donald Watt
The Spanish Civil War
Raymond Carr
Munich: Czech Tragedy
K.G.Robbins

Trevor Lloyd was born in London in 1934 and educated at Harrow and Merton College, Oxford. He is at present Associate Professor of History at the University of Toronto. He has published *The General Election of 1880, Canada in World Affairs 1957-59*, and *Empire to Welfare State*, a history of England in the 20th century.

JM Roberts, General Editor of the *Macdonald Library of the 20th Century*, is Fellow and Tutor in Modern History at Merton College, Oxford. He is also General Editor of Purnell's *History of the 20th Century* and Joint-Editor of the *English Historical Review*, and author of *Europe 1880-1945* in the Longman's History of Europe. He has been English Editor of the *Larousse Encyclopedia of Modern History*, has reviewed for *The Observer*, *New Statesman*, and *Spectator*, and given talks on the BBC.

Library of the 20th Century

Publisher: Iain Sproat
Editor: Jonathan Martin
Executive Editor: Richard Johnson
Assistant Editor: Jenny Ashby
Designed by: Brian Mayers/ Germano Facetti
Research: Germano Facetti/ Gunn Brinson

Pictures selected from the following sources:

Bath Academy of Art 71 81
Bertarelli 22
Brown Brothers 41 72 79 121
Caligari 35
Central Press 95
Communist Party (UK) 4 10 65
Crown Copyright 25
Culver Pictures 48 58 76 80 123
Dazy 50 65 92
Editions Rencontre 52
Fawcett Society 37 71 84 88 89 97 122
Guaita 1 10 23 26 100 110
L. Hine 33
Imperial War Museum 98 103 109
Le Rire 16 28 86
Library of Congress 20 24 34 38 41 74 75 79 80 86 120 121 122
London Museum 56 57 61 116 123
MalMaison (Versailles) 10
Mansell Collection 10 21 22 30 44 55 114 122 123
Musée de Saint-Denis 15
Museo de Milano 103
Museum Toulouse-Lautrec-Albi 8
Novosti 123
Odhams 92 93
Press Association 63
Radio Times Hulton 24 25 36 82 123
Raphael Tuck 112
Simplicissimus 128
Snark International 7 8 11 12 16 19 21 31 35 42 47 57 106
Sport and General 88
Syndication International 91
Ullstein 36 110 111
Victoria and Albert Museum 96
Viollet 6 113
Wallace Collection 11
Wohfeld 112

DATE DUE

The Absolutely Perfect Horse

The
Absolutely
Perfect Horse

by Marylois Dunn
with Ardath Mayhar

1 8 **f** 1 7

HARPER & ROW, PUBLISHERS

Cambridge, Philadelphia, San Francisco, London, Mexico City, São Paulo, Sydney

NEW YORK

Library of Congress Cataloging in Publication Data
Dunn, Mary Lois.
    The absolutely perfect horse.

    Summary: The formerly noble, now downtrodden horse known as Dogmeat helps Annie
and her family reassess their values.
    1. Horses—Juvenile fiction. [1. Horses—Fiction]
I. Mayhar, Ardath. II. Title.
PZ10.3.D883Ab 1983   [Fic]   82-47726
ISBN 0-06-021773-1
ISBN 0-06-021774-X (lib. bdg.)

The
Absolutely
Perfect Horse

1

The bill of sale said his name was Admiral Benbow. Nobody could ever figure out why, for he was never called that. The sideshow people called him Chief, to make him seem truly an Indian pony. I called him Dogmeat, for by the time he came to us that was all he was good for. And it was a more appropriate name for the bony old Appaloosa than my sister would ever admit.

He backed out of the trailer as confidently as if he were coming home, and later I realized that it was true. The old horse had found a home, at last . . . a home to die in. But first he made himself so much a part of the Braeden family that he will live as long as the last of us lives. Dogmeat was a different sort of horse.

He arrived late in the spring of the year I turned thirteen. By the time my birthday rolled around, I had aged a long way past any thirteen, and Annie, my fifteen-year-old sister, had grown up overnight. Looking back, I really don't understand how we had remained as childlike as we had, for there had been sudden and dramatic changes in our lives already.

The change had begun abruptly. Lieutenant Commander Kelley had come, himself, with the telegram announcing that our father had been badly injured while on duty in the Far East. Commander Kelley was a special friend of our family, and Annie and I had called him Uncle Ed ever since we could remember. We were lucky that that was so, because he didn't stop at breaking the news gently to us and Mother— he arranged to have Dad flown to the big hospital in Honolulu. Then he got Mother transport to go over and take care of him.

Not content with all that, he took us home with him, and we stayed there and went to school with his children for five months. That was a long five months. We seemed to be suspended somewhere unfamiliar, just going to school, then rushing home to see if there was a letter from Mom. I can still feel the warm glow I felt when she wrote, "Your father took a couple of steps today—all by himself."

Her letters were full of all kinds of interesting things as well as news of her patient. She loved the islands

4

and the people there, and she had known a lot of them before, when she and Dad had been stationed there. Mostly, though, she wrote about the boy who had saved Dad's life when his small boat had hit an old mine—heaven knows which war it was from—that had somehow gotten itself out into the river.

Taro Chan was the boy's name, but he wasn't Japanese. He was Vietnamese, actually, though his name had somehow come out as Japanese. Uncle Ed laughed when he said the name and told us it was the equivalent of John Doe in America. It was a funny name, but that was all I could see about him that was funny. You could tell from Mom's letters that she liked him a lot. When Taro Chan recovered from his wounds, and the government was going to ship him back to Thailand, where he and Dad had been hurt, she and Dad did a lot of talking and yelling and medal rattling. It was arranged that Taro Chan would stay on in Honolulu.

Mom came home plumper and rounder than I remembered. She was quick to wrap us in hugs, and I had to reach farther than ever before to get my arms around her.

"That's because there's going to be a baby," she said.

Annie was tickled to death. She was full of plans, right off. "We can take that little playroom and put all Petey's junk in the attic," she started.

"It's not junk, but you can put most of it away if you want to," I said. I really didn't care. Most of the stuff was toys I didn't have time for anymore. The games and things I really wanted could be stuffed under my bed or in the closet. I had a lot of old motorcycle magazines I could throw out to make room.

Mom sat down on the couch and patted the cushions on either side of her. We sat close, so she could hug and sit at the same time.

"The baby won't be the only new member of the family," she said. "Sam and I have decided to adopt Taro Chan. Most of the paperwork is already done, and we hope he can come home with your dad when he flies home."

I couldn't work up a lot of excitement about a little squally baby, as Annie could. Babies seem to interest girls a lot, I've noticed. Taro Chan was something else. A full-grown brother to play with! Though I wasn't sure, from what Mom had written, that he'd know very much about playing. He was no older than Annie, but he'd been a sailor in the Thai river fleet for several years already. He had fought Reds and even river pirates, she said. He could handle a boat as well as any man, and, to quote Dad, he "could come on real warlike when the occasion demanded." It would be something to have a Vietnamese brother, and a warrior, besides.

"We can put bunk beds in my room," I said. I was already planning to begin clearing out my room to make space . . . maybe that very afternoon.

"Well . . ." Mom sounded thoughtful. Her eyes

were hiding something from us, as if she were wondering how much news we could take all at the same time. "I don't think we'll worry too much about changing this house. We won't be living here much longer."

"Are we being transferred?" Annie asked. I don't ever remember being transferred. We had been when I was little, but we'd lived in this house for eight years, and it was all I could remember.

"Not transferred," Mom said. "Your father is going to retire from the Navy. He had some bad wounds and a lot of surgery. He can't handle anything but a desk job anymore, and that would kill him more surely than the mine almost did. You know him. If he's not out doing something active, he's miserable."

"But we own this house," Annie said. There was a quaver in her voice. "We'll have to change schools."

"I'm afraid so. Still, you'll finish out the year here and start the new school in September, so it isn't like beginning in the middle of a year. And houses can be sold as well as bought."

"Where are we going to move to?" I asked. I was doing my best to keep my own voice from quivering. I had never gone to school anywhere but here, and I didn't think I was going to like changing very much. From her expression, Annie wasn't either.

"Petey, you may not remember, but Annie does, I know. We used to go to Texas every summer to visit my mother and father on the farm." She looked at Annie, who nodded and tried to smile. Mom hugged her again. "That was a long time ago. When

Mother died, a year after my father, she left the farm to me. We've rented the land to tenants, but the old house is just like Mother left it."

"But a farm . . ." Annie was concerned. "Won't that be awfully hard work for Dad?"

"It's hard work," Mom agreed. "Sam may not be able to do the heavy work for a long time. Maybe not the hardest of it . . . ever. But if all of us pitch in, with Taro Chan and a good hired hand I think we can make it work. I used to be pretty good at keeping a vegetable garden and tending chickens and pitching hay, when I was a girl. I'll bet you don't know that I can still milk a cow!"

We both laughed.

"Mother," Annie said, "you never wear jeans, even. We have always had a maid. I didn't know you could do anything."

"Except cook," I interrupted. "You sure can cook good!"

Mom laughed with us, this time. "And can vegetables and make preserves and jellies. I can make quilts and our own soap, find wild things to eat and to cure illnesses with. Not to mention hunt quail and dress chickens for eating and a thousand country things you've never had a chance to do. It's going to be fun for us all."

I didn't think "fun" sounded like quite the word for it, but Mom sounded so eager for us to like her idea that it would have been impossible not to try to.

"What kind of farm is it?" I asked. We had studied

8

a bit about different kinds of farming in Social Studies.

"It used to be a dairy farm, when my father was alive," Mother said. "It's good pasture land, good hayfields. You know, your father was raised on a ranch in North Dakota. He knows a lot about cattle. Sam thinks we can start out and build a beef herd. It takes a while to begin making money out of it, but it's pretty steady once the income starts coming in and the herd is built up and self-sustaining. And it isn't nearly as physically demanding as most other kinds of farming. Not so much equipment is needed, either. That can run into money if you don't watch it."

"It'll be more like a ranch than a farm," Annie said. She smiled for the first time . . . a real smile, I mean. "Horses. There will have to be horses to work the cattle."

"Perhaps later. It's not like a big open range, Annie. There are only six hundred and forty acres, all broken up into fenced pastures. Sam will probably use a jeep or a tractor to take care of the livestock."

Annie's smile faded, and her face slid into lines of disappointment. "But I don't know why you couldn't have a riding horse," Mom added quickly.

Annie forgot all about changing schools and laying aside all her old friends. "Oh, Mom, really? A black horse with a white star and white stockings? That would be an Absolutely Perfect Horse!"

Seeing Annie bounce around on her end of the couch didn't surprise me very much. A horse of her own was Annie's dream. She read books about horses, went to movies about horses, collected pictures, magazines, and little statues of horses. The last time I counted, there were one hundred and eighty-three of the little statues. A hundred and eighty-four, if you counted the big jade horse Mom kept under the glass dome in the living room. It was really Annie's, but it was too precious to be hidden away upstairs.

Annie went away to camp in the summers so she could ride every day. When Mom took us to the park so Annie could ride, it always looked to me as if she rode at least as well as most of the TV cowboys.

"Well, I would rather have an absolutely perfect motorcycle, like a 750 Harley or BSA. Slightly used, of course," I butted in.

Mom gave us another squeeze. "If that's what it will take to make you happy, we'll see what can be done. It's a big thing to move away from everything, everyone you have ever known." She paused a moment, thinking. "You know, you'll have to be reasonable about things. Annie, you may never find a horse with those absolutely perfect markings. And Petey, if we could afford a cycle like that, you aren't big enough to handle it yet."

We both nodded. That was reasonable. Still, I could feel Mom working up to something else. The Zinger.

"You know how expensive everything is, what with inflation. The move is going to be a terrible strain on our resources." I nodded, and I could see Annie nodding, too. She felt the Zinger coming as well as I did.

"We'll be able to sell this house for a lot of money, but the old farmhouse will have to be fixed up a lot.

It has a huge attic that we plan to divide into two large bedrooms and a bath for you boys. The house will have to be reroofed, painted inside and out. New appliances, new plumbing . . . even new wiring will have to go into it.

"And that's only the house. The fences are all old and will have to be repaired or rebuilt entirely. So will the barn and the sheds. There will have to be a certain amount of new equipment, too, and with the cost of the livestock, that will take a bundle. Can you imagine the money that's going to cost us?"

"Lots!" I said.

"Do we have enough?" Annie asked doubtfully.

"Not to do everything all at once," Mom answered in a reassuring voice. "But once we sell this house, then with our savings, we can make a good start on the important things. First the house, making it livable, and then the livestock. The rest will come along, in time. Not too long, I should think."

"I have lots of money in the bank," I reminded her.

"Me, too," Annie said.

"Not your college money." Mom shook her head decidedly. "We aren't going to touch that. It will be more important than ever to leave your money alone. College will be coming up soon enough for you two, and you'll need everything you have, plus anything we can add to it. And Taro Chan will have to have a chance to go to school, too. Money is going to be a little short around here for a while."

Annie frowned. "If we don't have any money to

spend, how can we get Petey a cycle and me a horse?"

"Why, you already get an allowance. And when you work on the farm, you'll be paid for that, too. We don't tell you how to spend your allowances, and we won't tell you how to spend your salaries. If you want to spend what you get, fine. If you want to save for what you want, then that's even better."

"Wow!" I said. "I never made a salary before."

"Well, it won't be as much as a full-time, full-grown hired man would make, because you will be part owner of the farm, and you'll be working for yourselves, just as your father and I will. Still, it'll be a substantially larger amount than you're getting now."

"What about him?" Annie said, and I knew she meant Taro Chan. "Will he get an allowance too?"

"Of course," Mom answered. "Remember, Taro Chan is your adopted brother. You have to start thinking of him as a member of the family, not as an outsider. He's going to feel strange enough as it is, when he comes home."

I hugged her again. "I'm glad you decided to take him into the family," I said, hoping that she didn't notice that Annie just sniffed and didn't say a thing.

2

That was the day, I remember, when I started really thinking before I bought a comic book. *Do I want this now or a motorcycle later?* It had never occurred to me before to save money for one, because Mom would never have let me have one in the city. No more than she could let Annie have a horse on our roof garden.

That day, too, marked a change in Mom. Instead of deciding instantly, when Annie or I asked her about anything, she began to say, "We'll have to wait and ask your father." It seemed a little strange, for Dad had been gone a long time, and we were used to having Mom make all the decisions.

After a while, I figured that it was her way of easing

13

us into the habit of looking to Dad as well as to her for answers to our questions. Besides that, it was hard not to get the feeling that there were going to be a lot more changes coming about in our lives . . . aside from a big move and two new members added to the family.

The changes began with Dad's return. That was like a new beginning for everybody. He stood tall and straight in the door of the plane. Then he stepped slowly and carefully down the ramp to the spot where we waited. I could feel him controlling the need to limp. There was something about the set of his shoulders, the way he moved, that told me he was hurting. But he didn't limp, just made straight for us.

The ground was wet from showers that had fallen the night before, and everything smelled fresh and clean. Dad's uniform was as crisp as if it had just come off the hanger, and sunlight glittered on the gold trim and the clusters of ribbons on his chest. He was so thin; I didn't remember him as being so terribly thin. His smile was the same, though, curved like a sailing sea gull's wings.

He hugged and kissed Mom and Annie, then he held out his hand to me. I took it, and we shook hands, but I wanted to be hugged too, so I wrapped my arms around his waist, and he held me tighter than anyone else. Then he turned, one arm still heavy around my shoulders, and held out his free hand to the slim Oriental youth who had come down the ramp behind him.

14

"Annie, Petey, this is Taro Chan."

Strangely, I felt disappointed. From his name and the things Mom had told us in her letters . . . about what a soldier he was . . . I expected Taro Chan to be a Samurai sort of person. This slender, dark-eyed boy with the shy smile looked not very different from the boys in my class. His name didn't fit, either. There was nothing Japanese about him, unless it was his eyes. They were definitely Oriental, but the rest of him, face and all, was just like ordinary people.

"The Captain says I have good English," he said, holding out his hand to me. "I am please to becoming your brother."

He pronounced brother as "brudder," the way the Hawaiians did when they were talking to tourists. I didn't know if he always talked that way or if he was teasing. I took his hand anyway.

"Your English is good enough for us. It's going to be great to have another man on my side. I've always been outvoted by the women up to now."

Taro Chan looked with distress at Mom and Annie. "I do not think it is ever correct I should argue with the mother," he said.

Dad and I laughed, and Mother nodded. "You'll learn, my lad, when you've been around Annie and Petey for a while. You'll learn how, I'd bet on it." She kissed him on the cheek, and he blushed.

"You'll have to get used to that," I told him. "Mom's a hugger and kisser."

"I think I can get used to," he answered very seri-

15

ously. "I think I will like very much a hugger and kisser. It has been very long since my own mother is gone."

"Is she dead?" Annie asked, speaking to him for the first time.

"There is no way to know," he said. "I am very young when the war in Vietnam is over. My village is gone, I am left too young to know anything. The Americans find me, give me into care of nuns. They take me to Thailand. One of sisters was Japanese, Sister Toyoko. She name me Taro Chan, because I was too young to know my name. They give me home, while I am little. When I was older, I joined the river patrol. And that is how I met the Captain. Your father."

I could tell that he had rehearsed that speech many times. He would have realized that we would be curious about his past. Still, he seemed embarrassed. "I think I have answered more question than you have asked," he mumbled.

Dad shook him affectionately by the arm. "I think you saved yourself a lot of explaining. They'd have asked you questions all the way home, if I know those two. Now that's behind you. We can get on now to important things, like what's for lunch?"

As we walked back to the station wagon, Annie always kept Mother between herself and Taro Chan. Funny, I knew she didn't like the idea of adopting him, though she hadn't said a word after Mom broke the news. I know Annie pretty well. Still, I hadn't thought she was going to be afraid of him, and that was the way she was acting.

16

When we had a minute to ourselves at home, I asked her about it.

"I don't know, Pete." She seemed miserable and strange. "I can't explain it. I'm not exactly afraid of him, but he makes my skin crawl. I wish Dad hadn't brought him."

"Annie, he didn't have anyplace else to go except back to Thailand to get killed, sooner or later, on the river. And he did save Dad's life."

She shrugged and sighed. "I know that. I can't understand it, myself. Much less explain it to you. I just don't like him."

I could think of a lot of reasons to like Taro Chan, but it isn't any use arguing with feelings. They don't understand words.

"O.K.," I said. "Can you just be nice to him?"

"I'll try, Petey. I'll really try. But will you do something for me? Just keep him a good way from me until I have time to get used to having him around. Keep him busy."

Annie need not have worried. Time and the move across four states kept us too busy to think about anything except what to pack (or unpack) next. Unless you have moved, pulled up roots and shaken loose from everything you've ever known, leaving as exciting a city as San Francisco for a run-down farm in a pine forest, you would never understand the next few weeks we lived through.

If it hadn't been for Taro Chan—T.C., as he came to be called—we wouldn't have made it. He knew what to pack and where to put it as well as Mom and Dad did. We were all the time asking, "Where should this go? Does this need to be marked fragile?" He knew, without asking. And finally the movers loaded up the boxes and crates and hauled them away, while we followed at a more leisurely pace in the station wagon.

We managed to survive it all. The new sort of life; the old/new house; the baby, who came a bit sooner than he was expected. The small new schools, when September came, were not very different from the old schools, except for their looks. The new people were mixed—I guess most people are. Not only did we survive, it even seemed that Annie might be getting over her feelings about T.C.

Among all the rest, we were saving our money, remembering Mom's promise. And in the spring, Annie announced, "Daddy, I think I'm ready to buy my horse."

3

I woke up that morning as soon as Annie's feet hit the floor in her room across the hall. I didn't move, or open my eyes. I lay with all my senses alert to what was happening all around me, as T.C. had taught me to do. I was thankful all over again that we had kept the old farmhouse instead of tearing it down to build something in brick and plastic. The old cypress house communicated. It creaked and rattled in a different way to the step of each of us. It sounded different to the beat of a south wind, north, east, and west wind. It had its sunny-day sounds and its rainy-day sounds. It was full of special noises, all comfortable, settled-down sounds.

In a strange way, it was like the house we had left

in San Francisco. Not in looks. That had been a tall, narrow house right on the street. That house had always reminded me of a tall lady wearing a jaunty flowered hat, for the flowers in the roof garden always spilled over the railings, making ruffles of color that could be seen from the street. That had been a great house, with its view of the old orange bridge and the bay. I couldn't remember another. But this was a good house, too, full of Texas's past. If it had ghosts, they were friendly ones and didn't inflict any troubles they might have had on the new tenants.

The house was waking up. I could hear Dad's razor buzzing and the sound of his voice talking to the baby in mostly nonsense talk. I heard Annie go back to her room from the bathroom, and I swung down from the top bunk and carefully set one foot in the middle of T.C.

"Uhff!" he grunted. That was followed by what I took to be a choice Oriental obscenity, one of those he always refused to translate and that always made Dad's eyebrows go up when T.C. forgot and let loose in his hearing.

"Petey! What for you waking me up before the birds quit singing?"

"Annie's up. Come on! You want to come along, don't you?"

T.C. narrowed his eyes into slits, making him look like Confucius. "Not me, Petey. I saw all the horses I ever wanted to see last night. It was way after midnight when we got home. This is Saturday. Just leave, very quiet. Let the old man sleep in peace." He didn't,

I noticed, have much accent anymore unless he affected it.

"Peace, brudder," I said and yanked the covers over his head before going into the bathroom to pull on my jeans and the faded pink University of Southern California sweat shirt I was going to wear. Annie didn't particularly want either one of us to go along, I well knew, but I wasn't about to miss the auction or the chance to help her pick out the Absolutely Perfect Horse.

Downstairs in the kitchen, Mom rattled pots and pans, singing as she made breakfast. Dad's voice interrupted her, and she answered with a report of the correct time. I couldn't help laughing. The electricity must have gone off again. I could imagine Dad grumbling under his breath and saying that things just weren't run shipshape in the country. Not like he was used to in the Navy, at any rate. Of course, he usually finished up his grumbling with some tale of a colossal foul-up from his underwater-demolition-team days in the Korean War.

"Now there," he would say with his eyes sparkling with memory, "was a *real* mess."

It took Annie longer to dress, painting on an inch of black goop around her eyes and straightening her nice curly hair with one of those gunks the girls use, so I went on downstairs.

"Morning, Mom. Dad. Morning, Brad." I kissed the baby on top of his head and slid onto my place on the long bench behind the table. The baby squealed "Pee-Tee" in his high, wispy voice.

Mom turned from the bacon she was frying and smiled at both of us. "Morning, Petey. Go get the paper for me, will you?"

I slid out from behind the table and closed the kitchen door quietly behind me. I took two giant steps across the wide porch and one down the three wooden steps to the path. The yard just around the house was fenced. Beds of flowers bloomed everywhere inside the fence. Ouside, the tall grass was neatly mowed on both sides of the dusty road that curved away to meet the farm-to-market road where our mailbox and the paper box stood beside our gate. Our dirt road was a good quarter mile long, and a thick stand of trees filled the curve between our place and the main road. Sometimes there were owls in the trees early in the morning. Today, except for a mockingbird and a couple of cardinals, there was nothing. The small birds wouldn't have been singing if the owl had been around.

I picked up the paper and jogged back, puffing harder than was really necessary.

"Gracious me," Dad said with a quavery voice, as I puffed into the kitchen, "you are certainly out of condition, little boy. What we need around here is a mule and a plow. That would put some muscles into those weak and spindly little legs of yours."

"Uh-huh." I continued to puff, even though the need had passed. "Maybe Annie will buy us a good mule today, instead of that A.P.H. of hers."

Dad grinned and shook out the paper. "Not a chance, Petey, my lad. You can forget about that!"

"Now don't open that paper before you eat your eggs," Mom said, turning from the stove.

Annie came bounding down the stairs, sounding almost like the horse she had talked about so constantly. Brad began to beat on his chair, chanting, "Ann-ee, Ann-ee, Ann-ee!" as soon as he heard her coming.

She picked him up and whirled him around, hugging him tightly and planting a loud kiss on top of his red curls as she plopped him back into his high chair. He squealed with delight, bouncing up and down. Dad spared a hand from the paper to steady the chair.

"Brad thinks you look especially nice this morning, too," he said, grinning at Annie as she sat down.

"Flatterers!" she laughed. "The whole lot of you."

"I didn't say a word," I said, and she wrinkled her nose at me. It didn't hurt her looks any. Annie was a pretty girl. Her hair was an exact cross between Dad's black and Mom's red, which is a hard color to describe, but nice.

She tried all the tricks to make it smooth and straight as a string, the way the Pine Hill girls wore theirs, but she never quite succeeded. The natural waves would spring out, whatever she did. This morning she had parted it in the middle and tied the heavy falls on either side with leather thongs, Indian fashion. With the loose-sleeved shirt and cutoffs and Indian moccasins, Annie looked a little like an Indian girl. Too, she hadn't taken time to paint around her eyes. They looked like two regular eyes today, instead of two sapphires in a coal bin. She was wearing pale frosted lipstick, though, and I couldn't let that pass.

"Yecch! You look like a ghoul."

She stuck out her tongue, thought how childish that must look, and settled for a haughty frown. Dad's face took on the expression he had when he didn't want us to know he was laughing at us.

"Well, my little chickadee," he said in his famous (bad) imitation of W.C. Fields. "Ready to go?"

"I've been ready for days." Annie laughed, helping herself to eggs off the platter Mom set in front of her.

"Weeks," Mom corrected, kissing her on top of the head. "I haven't heard anything but horse, horse, horse, until I think we're all going to turn into horses."

"Oh, Mom!"

Dad laughed. "Altogether, I don't think Annie's mentioned horse but every other breath since she finally scrounged enough money for the A.P.H."

Mom finally sat down at the table and looked around. "Where's T.C.?"

"He said he'd seen enough horses at the show last night to last him awhile. He wants to sleep late, so he's not coming," I said.

Annie looked at her plate and continued eating.

"He told me last night that he had a lot of history to study today," Dad said, looking at Annie. When she didn't say anything, he sighed. "I guess it's just as well."

"Well, I can't imagine T.C. being very interested

in horses," Mom said. "Now if we were going after a motorcycle . . ."

Annie looked up and grinned across the table. "A tricycle for Petey, you mean."

I threatened her with a piece of buttered toast and had her laughing again. It seemed like a good idea to keep her in a good mood, since I knew she didn't really want me tagging along, either.

I watched as Annie sat chewing somewhat mechanically, her eyes glazed, as she went off into some part of her dream about the A.P.H. Probably the part where they were galloping, wild and free. Drumming swiftly over the little-used dirt roads, having adventures, just girl and horse. She had told me her dream often enough.

"Hey," Dad said for the third time before he finally got through to her. When her eyes unglazed, he said, "Your plate's been clean for ten minutes. We're ready whenever you are."

"Now!" She got to her feet eagerly. "I'm ready right now. Meet you at the truck."

There was no doubt about her excitement. When she came outside, clutching her purse, she climbed into the middle of the pickup seat without arguing about who was going to sit on the outside. I knew by that that she was excited. Mom stood away from the truck after Dad kissed her good-bye, and waved as we headed out toward the road. The single-horse trailer we had borrowed from the vet, Dr. Kurt, bounced easily behind.

As the pickup moved across the cattle guard and onto the hard-top road, Annie began to shiver. I had had those, too, at times. The kind of shivers that start at the front of your ribs and slide all the way down to your knees, one after the other. Dad felt them, too.

"Cold, Annie?"

"Gosh no. Scared, I guess."

Dad laughed, more sympathetic than amused, and shook his head. "I know the feeling."

Now that we were this far down the road, I decided it was safe to become a speaking member of the group. "After seeing all those gaited horses and those jumpers last night, what kind have you decided on this morning?"

Annie looked at me to see if I was teasing. I wasn't. Dad was looking straight ahead, wearing his "Captain" look, but a smile tugged at the corners of his mouth.

"This morning, I'm leaning toward a Tennessee Walking Horse, but I'd settle for a nice little Morgan or Arab. I think I'll just have to let my heart pick him out. I'll know him when I see him."

All the way to the fairgrounds, she talked about breeds and sizes, colors and markings, training and temperament. Annie had decided, after moving to Pine Hill, that she wanted a mare or a gelding, because stallions generally are not as companionable on rides with groups, and she wanted to be a part of the group rides that her school friends took on most weekends. She was going to look for a comfortable horse, sleek and perky, affectionate and gentle. A horse she wouldn't have to fight every inch of the way. She wanted a friend who would go because he liked to go and because he liked her.

Of course, if he happened to be black with white stockings and a white star, that would be *great*. The Absolutely Perfect Horse. Dad and I had heard the whole tale many times before, but it helped to pass the time.

The Horse Fair was an annual event in Pine Hill. It was the big event of the community. Horsemen came from as far away as Mexico, Canada, California, and Tennessee to show and sell their horses. The horse show that ran at the same time gave them a chance to show their animals' paces and talents. As well as entertaining all comers, it helped to raise the prices of the best animals.

There were classes for all kinds of show horses, performance classes for the working breeds, and halter and equitation classes for children. But the big drawing card was the auction in the afternoon of the final day. There were a lot of horse shows around the country, but very few auctions like this one were held.

Some of the mounts to be sold were prizewinners that would sell for unbelievable prices. I couldn't understand, myself, why anybody would spend more than a thousand dollars on a horse. But fortunately for Annie, there were also ordinary horses for ordinary people at ordinary prices.

4

The parking lot at the fairgrounds was dusty. Cars and pickups, most of them pulling one-, two-, or even four-horse trailers, were gradually melding into featureless lumps, under a coating of the iron-red dust. The work T.C. and I had done in washing and polishing the truck and trailer was going to be wasted. From the scummy look of most of the trailers, nobody else had bothered. Not one seemed to have started the morning as clean as our trailer, or lined at the bottom with fresh hay for the new occupant.

Performance classes were still going on, but Annie said she'd seen enough of that last night at the show. "Let's go down to the barns," she said. "Maybe we can see the horses that are already tagged for sale."

From the looks of the crowds around the barns, a lot of other people had had the same idea. Annie looked at the milling people and pulled Dad toward a shadowy corner of the barn.

"Would you hold this for me, Daddy?" she asked, handing him the leather pouch that held her money.

"You sure?" he asked, hefting it.

"I'd feel better," she answered. "Some of the characters I see around here look pretty raunchy."

He nodded. "O.K., honey. Anybody snatches my purse will get fallen on. Heavily." He tied the strings together and slipped the loop over his belt; then he tucked the pouch under shirt and belt, pulling it around so that the slight bulge didn't show.

"That ought to be safe," he said. "You bring the whole wad?"

"No. One seventy-five. The rest is for feed and stuff."

I forgot about being invisible and snorted, "You won't get a prize Arab with that!"

Dad squelched me with a raised eyebrow. "We should get a pretty fair country riding horse for that," he said calmly.

Annie smiled at him, ignored me, and started down the long, dark corridor of the horse barn. Invisible was better. I dropped a few paces back, but Dad waited for me to catch up.

"Look, this is Annie's day, pal. Don't forget it again, see?" He did a swell Edward G. Robinson, but Little Caesar wouldn't have shaken a guy affectionately by the back of the neck and mussed his hair.

29

"I see."

As I walked along the stalls slowly, it was easy to match Dad, stride for stride. When he got into a hurry, forget it. Even with his bad leg, I couldn't keep up with him then.

Annie stopped to look at a four-year-old Morgan bay, who seemed nervous, tossing his head and gnawing at the boards on his stall. "That's a bad habit," she observed.

Dad pointed out a nice-sized pinto with a roached mane. "He looks likely."

"Look at his front legs. They both come out of the same sprocket-hole. I'd like a little more brisket," Annie decided, after walking around him for the fifth time.

The sorrel gelding had a milky cast in one eye, and the big roan was Roman nosed and, as his handler finally admitted, hard mouthed.

"Gee, Daddy, none of the horses in my price range are anything like I'm looking for, except maybe the gray Arab." Annie sounded disappointed.

The gray was pretty, even to me. He was five, a good age, and he bowed his neck and lipped carrot slices daintily out of Annie's hand. He had small ears that almost touched at their points, so steep was their arch, when he looked at something with interest.

"We hope to get five hundred for him," his owner said. And that wasn't even a prize horse.

"We're all hot and thirsty. Let's get a cool drink and set a spell, as the natives say, before the auction starts," said Dad, seeing her disappointment.

I agreed, fanning myself with some straw for emphasis. "Those poor horses in the show ring must be dying from the heat," I said. "It's awfully hot for May."

"O.K.," Annie said, agreeable for once. "I saw a booth down there about two barns away." She pointed with her chin. But she didn't have to point; we found the booth by the smell of barbecue cooking on the open grills.

"Is it too early for a sandwich?" I asked Dad.

"Not too early for me," he said and looked at Annie. "How about you?"

"Not too early for me, either. I can't even remember eating breakfast."

A dusty-looking man sat beside me and ordered a sandwich. "You folks come far?" he asked Dad.

"No. Not too far," Dad said. "We're the Braedens. Have a farm out of town about ten miles."

The man nodded and held his hand out to Dad across me, almost knocking my sandwich out of my hand. "I'm Tom Blackburn. Heard about you folks moving onto the old Johnson place. Raising cattle, ain't you? Going in for horses, too, or just looking around?"

"I'm Sam Braeden. These are my children, Pete and Annie," Dad said. "We came to buy Annie a horse."

"But we haven't seen anything I like. At least not anything I can afford," she said.

"What kind of horse you looking for?" he asked.

"A nice riding horse," she said. "But everything

31

seems to be show horses. Not just horses for people to ride for fun."

"Yeah, " he agreed. "I'm looking for a good woods horse myself. Something with good shoulders and enough heart to jump logs and gullies. I raise coon dogs. Sometimes the only way to follow them is on horseback."

"Have you been through all the barns?" Annie asked.

"No. Some of 'em. But don't be discouraged if you don't see just what you're looking for in the barns. All the sale horses aren't in those stalls. Some are still in trailers. There are probably quite a few that won't be tagged until this afternoon. And besides"— he smiled—"bid what you can afford to pay on any horse that takes your fancy. You never can tell. You might get a bargain. A real bargain. It has happened."

Mr. Blackburn slid off his stool, his sandwich finished. "See you folks around."

After he was gone, Annie seemed more cheerful. Probably dreaming about maybe owning that pretty gray Arab.

"If the horses won't even be tagged until this afternoon, let's go look at the sideshow," I said. I was tired of looking at horses.

The big carnival was as much a part of the horse fair as the horses. The kids at school talked a lot about the shows from previous years. There had been twin dog-faced boys, a man who ate light bulbs and razor blades, a fat lady with a red beard, magic shows, and one tent kids didn't get into where ladies took off their clothes to music.

We played some of the gyp games that Dad called "ponies" and ate popcorn while we worked our way down the midway toward a long tent that stood apart from the others.

INDIAN MUSEUM, its banner proclaimed. GENUINE ARTIFACTS OF THE EARLY WEST. INDIAN MUMMY. Original costume worn by CHIEF CRAZY HORSE at LITTLE BIG HORN MASSACRE. GENUINE GENERAL CUSTER'S GENUINE SADDLE. SEE THE NECKLACE made of the KNUCKLEBONES OF CUSTER'S TROOPERS. THOUSANDS OF GENUINE ARTICLES of the *EARLY WEST.*

"Can we go into this one, Daddy? It looks pretty good." It was the first interest Annie had shown since we left the barns.

"I can hardly wait to see Custer's saddle," Dad said, very wryly. "It must have had a nail in it pointing the wrong way, or the old boy wouldn't have been so proddy."

The only museum that would interest my dad was one about ships and Navy stuff, but he paid the tired-looking man at the front entrance.

As the tall guy handed out the mimeographed guidebooks, I looked him over. He was the tallest man I had ever seen. Dad was over six feet by a couple of inches or so, but this guy was at least a head taller. Only he kind of slumped over and let

33

his shoulders round off, something my dad would never do. *He* was as straight as a mainmast.

The tall man had a black-and-white badge pinned on his shirt. It said WALKER, and I guessed that was his name. He seemed uninterested in us until Annie walked past him. He reached out and touched one of her pony tails with a not-too-clean finger.

"Say," he said. "I just lost my Indian Maiden. Don't suppose you'd be interested?"

Annie and I both looked at Dad, whose eyebrows were climbing.

The tall man saw the expression too and muttered, "No. I suppose not," to answer his own question.

"But thank you very much for asking me," Annie said. "Nobody ever thought I looked like an Indian Maiden before." Annie's not always too smart, but she *is* polite.

"You look more genuine than most of my artifacts," the man said, nodding toward the tent. "And a whole heap better than the Indian pony the Maiden is supposed to ride."

Annie's face fell, and I must have showed my disappointment too, because Walker hastened to add, "Oh, they're genuine enough. But old, real old. They've been carried around a lot, and that wears on an exhibit real bad."

"Custer's saddle, too?" Dad asked. From his tone, I knew he didn't think it really was Custer's saddle.

"Well"—the man scratched his head, judging us shrewdly with his pale eyes to see how much we could be expected to swallow. "It was bought in South Da-

34

kota from a man who swore he got it off the Indian who took it from Custer's dead horse. Nobody could be positive. Them Indians lie a lot. But it's fancier than most. Not issue McClellan, for sure. Got his monogram burned into the leather. It's most likely his saddle, all right."

Dad didn't say anything but took each of us by the arm and walked us into the tent. The man called after us with a weary note in his voice, "Let me know how you like the exhibit."

"A tourist trap, Daddy?" Annie asked. We had learned long ago about those crummy "museums" that line the highways of the far west. Very few of them have anything worth the price of admisssion. Mostly they are full of cheap plastic "souvenirs" that have nothing to do with the location they're supposed to remind you of and are just the same cheap things you saw in the last museum, with a different decal stuck on. Even I had outgrown that junk.

"Maybe. Maybe not. We'll see," Dad said.

5

It was and it wasn't. Most of the things in the illuminated glass cases looked dusty. The mummy looked even drier than a mummy ought to look. Many of the arrowheads in the cases had slipped out of their positions on the glued-down patterns and lay in the bottom, helter-skelter.

The beaded buckskins marked CRAZY HORSE BATTLE DRESS were much more elaborate than any of my reading would lead me to think that a chief would wear into battle.

"I always thought Indians went into battle pretty near naked," I said.

"So did I," Dad agreed.

The most interesting thing, to me, was the necklace

made out of finger bones, supposedly from the trigger fingers of Custer's men. It was gruesome. The bones were drilled through the top and hung down the long way. In between the longer finger bones were some small grayish beads or bones, round ones. There were more than thirty finger bones, but Annie pulled me away from the case before I finished counting.

Maybe this would be a good place to explain about me. I like to count things. I don't know why, I just do it. I count cows in the fields as we drive along. I count fence posts, telephone poles between towns, rosebuds on the new bushes in Mom's flower beds. I knew to the dot how many holes were in the ceiling tiles of my classroom and how many ceiling tiles were in the school building. I knew how many light bulbs were in the fixtures in the church, how many bricks were in the chimney at home.

I like to count things because numbers are definite and solid, and I like good hard facts. Not many people go for that explanation, though, and Annie usually would get exasperated with me when she wanted to move on and I stood there counting something.

"Come on, Petey. Look at the saddles," she said. "There must be two hundred of them."

There weren't two hundred. There were only ninety-three, not counting Custer's, which was in a case by itself. It was fancy, all right. Too fancy. It looked more like pictures of the gear used by Spanish hidalgos. It had those fancy leather covers over the stirrups, and silver, lots of silver, all over it.

The rest of the saddles were behind a single strand

of rope. They sat on wooden frames, and every kind of saddle I had ever seen pictures of or read about seemed to be there. There were some I never imagined. Regular-issue McClellans, sidesaddles of many kinds, early Spanish ones with rusting iron stirrups and high backs. Cowboy saddles so high in front and back that it was easy to see how a man could ride for days on a cattle drive and sleep on his moving horse.

There were pack saddles, English flat saddles, early American saddles without horns, right on up to the modern calf ropers that aren't much but horn and stirrups. The rich, oiled-leather smell was a contrast to the dankness of the exhibit cases.

The saddles ended at the exit door, and the sunlight outside was so bright that for a moment we just stood blinking, trying to regain our vision. Annie got hers back first, or maybe it was instinct that took her to the little corral just outside the exit.

"Look. It's the genuine Indian pony," she said.

"How many Indians do you know who plow?" Dad asked her.

Annie looked at the horse seriously, as she did at all horses. "I don't think he's a plow horse. See, he has old saddle galls on his back and belly, but no harness marks anywhere. On an old fellow like him that would show."

Something did show. He was old, a real nag. His striped hooves were huge and cracked. The only shoe he had on was loose, and it clacked when he walked over to the fence to beg for sugar. His knees were knobby-looking, with bald patches. The upper legs were chunky, and the shoulders and hips seemed flat and kind of hollowed out where they should have been fat. The backbone was pretty straight, but it was sharp, and his ribs were easy to count. His neck was hollow, too, and seemed almost too skinny to hold up his head. Still, the head itself was reasonably good-looking.

For one thing, he looked smart. He had small, cleanly shaped ears that would have been nice if he had held them up instead of letting them flop tiredly in different directions. The eyes were nice, too, dark and clear, with no white showing in the eye, just a small outline around it.

His nose wasn't runny like those of some of the horses we'd looked at, but his large nostrils were just about as funny-looking. I didn't like the way his lower lip hung loose under his chin, either.

"It gives him a sad, hopeless expression," I said.

He was dusty, like everything else at the fair-grounds, but beneath the dust was a faded brownish color with big white spots on his behind. His mane and tail were turning gray from their original color. The were still long and silky-looking, though. Old, yeah, but pretty nice-looking, all in all.

Annie gave me a couple of carrot slices, and I held them out to him. He pushed them around my palm with velvet-covered lips and dropped them in the dirt.

"I don't think he has enough teeth to chew with."

"He likes us," Annie said, reaching through the fence to scratch behind his ears. The old horse sighed noisily and moved closer to the fence so she could reach him better.

"I don't think he can chew carrots," I said again. "Don't you have any sugar?"

Annie brought sugar from another pocket, and the old horse lifted the cubes carefully from her hand. None of them dropped to the ground.

"At his age," she said, "I don't suppose it matters that sugar isn't good for his teeth."

"No teeth," Dad said. "Good thing, too. You guys are going to put out your hands to a strange horse one day, and draw back bloody stumps."

"Oh, no. Not this fellow," Annie crooned in the voice she reserved for the baby and assorted visiting children.

Dad waited patiently, as we patted the old horse. "Don't you think we'd better get a seat? It's twelve-thirty. Auction ought to be starting soon, Annie," he finally said, when he was tired of waiting.

From behind us at the exit door of the tent the tall man said, "He's a friendly old cayuse. I'm going to miss him, in a way."

Annie, who had just about caught up with Dad and me, stopped and turned back. Dad sighed and stopped, shifting from foot to foot wearily. His leg hurt when he stood too long.

"Is he the Indian Maiden's horse?" she asked.

Walker laughed. "The Indian Maiden never saw a horse until she came to work for me. She wouldn't even feed the old Chief here if I didn't make her do it. Reckon he's one of the reasons she took off."

40

"If she's not taking him, why are you going to miss him?" Annie asked persistently.

"Look at him. I need a more likely-looking horse. What better place to get one than at an auction? I saw a little pinto over there, ought to go cheap. He won't be much of a using horse, but he's flashy and that's what I need."

"What are you going to do with *him*?" Annie sounded suspicious. "Sell him at the auction?"

Walker laughed again. "Why, missy, they'd plumb laugh me out of the arena. No, I called some people I know to come pick him up. He's no good for anything but dogmeat anymore."

Annie gasped and turned to Dad. She didn't say anything out loud. She didn't have to.

"Now, Annie. We're just a one-horse farm. Not a home for worn-out Indian ponies." He turned to Walker. "If you'd feed him once in a while, maybe he wouldn't be so worn out."

The tall man sighed. "It ain't that, mister. Don't get huffy. I treat him good. He didn't never eat elegant, but neither do I. He eats plenty, he's just plain old. I got papers that show he's coming nigh onto thirty-five. I got to have a horse with a little spunk. Something to catch the kiddies' eyes when the Indian Maiden rides him down the midway."

Annie reached out and put her hand on Dad's arm, but she was talking to Walker. "How much do the dogmeat people pay?"

"One horse, Annie," Dad said. "One horse is all we have room for, and one horse is all we are going

41

to get. This old fellow is dead on his feet. Come on, let's go to the auction."

"I don't want to go to the auction, Daddy. This is the horse I want."

I was too stunned to snicker. This old beat-up bundle of bones was as far from the A.P.H. we had heard so much about as it was possible to get.

"No, missy," the tall man said, sounding concerned. "You get on over to the auction with your dad. A pretty little lady like you needs a perky little horse to ride. You couldn't never ride this old fellow. Why, his heart nearly pounds out of his chest when he walks from the corral to the trailer. He ain't no horse for you."

I walked back to Annie and tugged her arm. "Come on, Annie . . . the auction'll be starting. You might miss a chance at a good horse."

She didn't answer me, just gently lifted her arm away from my hand. Annie was so much like Mom sometimes, it was spooky. She had that strange set look Mom gets sometimes when she's determined to do something and is just a little scared it might not be the right thing. Dad called it Mom's Irish streak . . . "*Mad* Irish streak" was the way he actually put it.

I noticed that he'd seen Annie's expresson, too, and I tried again. "Annie, that's been a good old horse, but he's sure not the A.P.H. Let's go look at that gray Arab again. Maybe he'll go for just what you want to pay.

She turned back to Walker and said, "How much?"

"Never you mind," the tall man's voice was sharp now. "He ain't for sale to you. I done called the dogmeat people. You go on over to the auction and get your Ayrab. I might even see you over there after the truck comes. I got to get me another Indian pony."

Annie ignored me, looked at Dad. "Daddy, I know I can't have another horse. You said I could have any horse I could afford. I want this one."

Dad threw up his hands in defeat. "Little-Mother-of-the-World wants the horse," he said to Walker. "How much?"

6

Walker looked at both of them. He thought they were crazy, I could tell. He didn't include me in his look because he could see I was on his side. In Dad's shoes, I'd have dragged the girl away from there kicking and screaming, if I'd had to, after all we'd heard about the Absolutely Perfect Horse. For some reason of his own, Dad had decided to let her make her own decision, however dumb it might be.

"Man, I don't like to tell you," Walker said. "They give me what he's worth in dogmeat. Twenty-five dollars. But he's not worth that as a keeping horse."

Dad pulled the pouch from under his shirt and belt and peeled off a twenty and a five. "Make out a bill of sale while I get the trailer," he said, turning on his heel and striding off. The set of his shoulders made me feel small and empty inside.

Now that it was done, Annie looked scared. She climbed inside the corral with the old horse and put her arm over his neck.

Walker looked at me and shook his head, looking from me to the money in his hand, to the girl and the horse. "Takes all kinds," he said at last and disappeared into the tent to get the bill of sale.

I climbed onto the fence and hung my arms over the top rail. "Annie . . ."

"I don't want to talk about it, Petey," she said.

She stood, rubbing the horse's forehead with her left hand and the soft spot under his jaws with her right. The old nag leaned against her with his eyes half closed. If he'd been a cat, he'd have purred.

From the tent came the sound of laughter and voices, as a group of visitors drifted out into the sunshine. I didn't have to see them to know that one of them was Cathy Thompson. She wasn't one of Annie's friends . . . or anybody else's. She was always in the middle of any group of people, her high-pitched, supersweet voice soaring above all the others. She was the high school bulletin board. Annie looked kind of sick.

"Well, well. Look who's tending the livestock. Hi, Annie. Who's your friend?"

"Hello, Cathy." I thought Annie used remarkable restraint in her tone. "Meet the Chief."

Cathy sniffed. "Chief? That's the genuine Indian pony? Looks more like the sole survivor of the Custer

Massacre." She pronounced the last word mas-sa-CREE, with a contemptuous twang. Two others in the group laughed. Ross Blackburn was wrapped around Cathy like a vine around a tree, and Tanya Bale, the Genuine Beauty Queen, was just behind them. But the slender, dark-haired boy who walked beside Tanya didn't laugh. He glanced at his friends impatiently and smiled at Annie. A nice smile, not a snicker.

When you're just a kid in junior high, the high school kids mostly don't seem to know you're around—or even alive. Tanya and some of Annie's other friends had been to our house several times, but I didn't remember them ever saying so much as hello to me. Evan Christophoulis was different.

From the first time he had delivered the groceries from his father's store to our house and discovered that T.C. was Vietnamese, a foreigner, they'd been friends. Perhaps it was because he was a Greek-born naturalized citizen. Or maybe he was just friendly. Anyway, he took T.C. as his special project. He took him places: movies and ball games; worked out on the farm with us when his father could spare him at the store; tutored T.C. when school started, in the subjects that were hard for him. English and history, mainly. T.C. didn't need any tutoring in math and science. He could hold his own there.

I liked Evan. He treated me as if I were a real person, not a younger brother. I was almost as tall as he was, standing on the lower rail of the fence. Evan hung his arms over the top rail, too.

"Hi, Petey," he said and nodded toward the Chief. "Seems nice and gentle."

Tanya tugged at him to pull him away from the fence. "Asleep, you mean."

Annie didn't say anything else. Hoping they'd go away, I suspect. She didn't mention that the horse was hers, which wasn't at all strange. A horse like that would take some explaining, and Annie would rather do it herself than have Cathy bray it all over school.

They turned to go, each couple arm in arm, but they had to stop as a stake-bed truck pulled up to the corral, raising clouds of dust. Before the dust even started to settle, an unshaven man in a torn khaki shirt and dirty pants stepped down.

Without his saying a word, I knew this was the dogmeat man. Annie knew it too. She was pale and really frightened-looking. Walker said he had called them, but somehow I never expected to see them. The old horse raised his head and peered forward expectantly. A truck to him meant moving on. He didn't know it would have been his final trip.

"That the horse?" the dirty man asked, and spat tobacco juice expertly over the fence between the animal's front hooves.

Annie stiffened and stood closer to her horse. "No, he's not. I mean he's the horse you came to get, but you can't have him now."

"Look-a-here. I know this seems bad to a kid, but the old nag won't never know the difference. Look at him. I'm doin' him a favor."

47

The man was opening the corral gate and moving inside as he spoke. He took hold of the halter. "Just move away now, and I'll get him loaded."

Without turning my head, I knew that Evan had come back and was standing beside me at the fence, not saying a word. It was like one of those nightmares when everything moves in slow motion. Annie moved as if her body were encased in cold honey. Even her speech seem slower.

"You can't take him," she said.

The man started to push her away and lead the old horse out of the corral. I was aware that Evan was no longer beside me, but in the corral behind Annie.

"I wouldn't," he said.

The trucker stared. Evan's move had been so easy and quiet that it occurred before anyone knew it was happening. Now Evan stood there, just behind Annie, balanced on the balls of his feet, flipping an empty Coke bottle up into the air and catching it by the neck, as it came down. The action was both graceful and strangely menacing.

"You keep out of this, kid," the trucker said, angry, now. "I was called to come git this nag, and I'm gonna git him." He reached again for the halter he had dropped when Evan vaulted the fence. Annie had hold of it now, and she wasn't about to let it go. I could see our pickup coming and I knew she could, too.

"Ease off, friend," Evan said, still flipping the Coke bottle and not raising his voice a hair. "The little lady doesn't want you to lay hands on her horse."

48

The trucker made a "come here" motion at the cab of the truck. A man who had been sitting slumped in the front seat unfolded from the right-hand side and slammed the door loudly as he came around the front of the cab.

"You havin' trouble, Frank?" he asked in a growly voice. There was an air of violence about him that made me shiver. He was big, a head and shoulders taller than Evan.

But if his size worried Evan, Evan didn't let it show. He continued to smile a gentle half smile, and the Coke bottle never missed a flip. Ross came over to the corral and began to climb the fence slowly. Cathy tugged at him, saying, "Keep out of this. That old nag isn't worth fighting about."

The trucker nodded in her direction. "Listen to your friend, there. This old horse is nearly gone. It'll be a mercy to let me take him. Now don't you two give me any more trouble. I'll just take that horse and be on my way."

"I've already bought him. You can't have him," Annie said. "Just because he's old, he's not useless."

"He ain't useless at all." The trucker grinned at her. "He'll make good dogmeat. That's useful." Then his smile faded, and his eyes narrowed. "What do you mean, you've already bought him?"

When the trucker had laughed about dogmeat being useful, Evan's smile froze. The bottle stopped flipping. He just held it loosely by its neck.

"She's bought the horse, friend. She isn't going to sell it to you. Now get out of the corral." He

49

didn't raise his voice, but I was shivering just the same and hanging on to the fence tightly, wishing Dad would hurry.

"Look, kid. We don't want trouble, but we came thirty miles out here to pick up this dogmeat, and I done told you two or three times. We're goin' to git him."

The big man was beside the trucker, now. Behind them, Dad stopped the pickup beside their truck. I didn't see him step down, but there was no mistaking his voice when it cracked across the corral like a whip. "What's the trouble, Annie?"

"This is the dogmeat man, Daddy. He won't believe that I've bought the horse."

The two men turned when Dad spoke. As they parted, I could see that he was poised just inside the gate. I'd never seen him look like this. His shoulders were squared and slightly forward, and his feet were evenly placed, but slightly apart, as if he were ready to jump forward or to either side. He gave the impression of being crouched to fight. From his expression, I thought he might welcome a chance to swing at somebody.

Evan began the slow flip, flip of the Coke bottle again. The grin returned to his lips. The odds had evened up.

"Mister, you'd better believe it," Dad said, in that tone that officers and schoolteachers develop early in their careers, if they are to be successful. "I don't know what my daughter sees in that old horse, but

50

she wants him, and she's paid for him. Take your argument up with the man who used to own him."

The trucker and his partner looked at each other and shuffled their feet, uncertain, now, of their position. "Look, I don't know anything but what I'm told. Walker called on the phone and said to come get the horse. I pay good money, and I had a long trip out here. I ain't trying to steal the horse."

"Go inside and get Walker, Annie," said Dad.

"Get Walker for what?" The tall man came out of the tent. "Uh-oh!" he said, as his eyes adjusted to the glare, and he took in the situation. "I thought you might get the old Chief away before they got here."

"Well, what did you call *me* for?" The trucker was angry, and he wasn't afraid to show Walker that he was.

"Never occurred to me that somebody might want the old Chief. The little lady wants him. Paid just what you'd have paid. Reckon he's her horse."

The trucker cursed briefly but choked off his outburst when he looked at Dad. He motioned his helper out of the corral, and they waited for Dad to move away from the gate. Neither of them seemed to want to shove past him. When they were both in the truck, Dad turned and watched them until they were out of sight. They clashed their gears as they drove away.

I was shivering, and Annie looked as if she would have fallen down without her firm grip on Chief's mane.

"You O.K.?" Dad asked Annie, though his glance included me.

"Sure." She nodded. "Fine, now. I certainly was scared there for a while, though. I thought he was going to take the horse in spite of anything I said."

"Hey, evzone," Dad said, holding out his hand to Evan. "Thanks for stepping in."

Evan flipped the Coke bottle to his left hand. He gripped Dad's hand with his right. "T.C. said sometimes you were twelve feet tall. I never saw it before today."

Dad was pleased. He grinned at Evan and said, "Now, now. You know I'm a peaceful man!"

"Yeah," Evan agreed. "Real peaceful."

From across the fence Tanya said, "Evan, come on!"

"Yes, come on. Evan, Ross! We've still got a lot of things to see and do this afternoon," Cathy called.

And tell, I thought.

"Thank you, Evan," Annie said.

He just smiled at us, as if nothing had happened and we were passing in the hall at school. Then he put his hands on top of the fence and vaulted it again, light as a feather. He ran a hand over my hair, standing it on end, as he turned away. "I thought you were in a hurry," he said to Tanya. "Let's stop by the Coke stand. I'd like to drop off this empty and get another. It's a very warm day."

7

I climbed down from the fence and let down the tail-
gate of the trailer. Then I went into the gate to stand
beside Dad. He was talking with Walker. Although
the whiplash was gone out of his voice, I could tell
he was still annoyed . . . as much at himself as at
anyone.

"You said you'd called them. It just didn't soak
into me that you'd committed the horse to them."

"I thought you'd be gone with the Chief before
they got here. . . . I'm sorry about the trouble, Mr.
Braeden. Old Chief's been with me a long time. Guess
I wanted you folks to have him, instead of them, even
if he ain't good for much."

"He'll be all right," Annie told him. "I'll take very good care of him."

"He ain't sick, missy," Walker said. "Just old and wore out. I doubt there's much you can do to build him up, but I'm glad he's going to a good home. He deserves it."

Annie lifted the old horse's head, almost holding it up by main strength with the worn halter he was wearing. She started leading him to the trailer. Walker stopped her. "Here," he said. "I reckon he's earned these things. He's wore 'em long enough."

He pulled a beaded bridle with a straight snaffle bit from its peg on the fence and handed it to Annie. Then he took the light Indian-design blanket and fastened it around the Chief with a wide surcingle, which had little stirrups attached. The old horse held his own head up once the gear was on; he thought, perhaps, that it was time for the show. He didn't even know that the big show had already taken place.

"A few Indian Maidens back, we used to rope off him some. He was real flashy then, but past his prime for cow work. He had some good years in the rodeo, I'm told. We had to quit roping with him, though. His legs just gave out on him. About a hundred yards is all he's good for, missy. I hope you won't be sorry you got him."

Walker helped Annie mount. "Ride him around a bit, then he'll think the show's over. He'll go right into the trailer. He's a good traveler. Had lots of practice."

Annie looked good on the horse, and he looked

better, too. While he was being ridden he didn't look so dopey. He lifted his big feet high and gave his head little tosses, like an actor trying to hog attention. I wondered if the saddle blanket was enough to pad away the sharpness of his backbone and ribs. When he shifted leads, I could see the muscles pull along his thin shoulders and hips.

Annie rode slowly around the corral several times before she nodded to me. I pushed the gate open, and she rode him into the trailer. I thought that was dumb, but it turned out to be safe enough. The old horse was trailer wise. He stood still, without breathing, until he felt Annie catch hold of the high side and pull herself off his back. Then he heaved a tremendous noisy sigh and relaxed, cock hipped, his head drooping almost to the hay-covered floor.

He was the picture of someone who has done a hard day's work and needs a long sleep to recover from it. Annie pulled his head up long enough to substitute the halter she had brought for the new horse, in place of the beaded bridle. She hung that on a peg, strapping it down with the chap strap that was there for the purpose. In an open trailer, gear can fly out if it's not carefully attached. Especially when it's light stuff.

While Annie rode, I listened to Walker tell Dad about the old Chief. He really was an Indian pony, born in the herd at the Blackfoot reservation in Montana. He had been trained for calf roping by a Blackfoot boy who wanted to follow the rodeo circuit. The colt had been smart and flashy and big enough to throw the heaviest calf. Finally, when the offers of big money for the horse got to be too much for the boy, who wasn't doing well as a rodeo performer, he sold him. The horse went through a series of owners, some good ropers, some poor ones, until he was too old for the arena.

Walker had been with a little carnival at the Chief's last rodeo, and he heard he was going to be sold for very little. He bought the horse, worked him easy, made a kind of pet out of him. The animal was affectionate and liked children. When the Indian Maiden rode him down the midway, all dressed up in her buckskins, they usually drew a good crowd back to the exhibit.

Dad shook hands with Walker when he was sure Annie had the loading completed.

"I'll take good care of him, Mr. Walker. He'll have a good home," Annie called again from the pickup.

"I know you will, missy. Thank you," Walker called back as we slowly pulled toward the road.

I stuck my head out of the window and waved. He waved back. The tall man stood there until the dust and a curve in the road put him out of my sight. The last I saw of him he looked more bent over than usual . . . bent and very sad.

There wasn't much to say. Annie had a horse. About as far from the A.P.H. we had started out to buy as it was possible to be. What had come over Annie to make her insist on that poor bony creature in the trailer behind us I would never figure. One thing I knew for sure. Anything I said would be wrong, so

I managed to keep quiet while four or five hundred questions marched around inside my head.

Dad broke the silence, after a bit, by clearing his throat and saying, "Well, Annie. You've got your horse."

"Daddy, when Dr. Kurt comes over to get his trailer this evening, I'll talk to him. He can tell me what to feed the Chief, how to take care of him."

"Annie," said Dad in a very gentle voice, "I talked with Mr. Walker while you were riding. The horse is at least thirty-five years old. Probably more. That's about a hundred and fifty years for a person. Horses and people just don't ordinarily live that long. I think you'd better realize for now and always that he isn't going to get well. He isn't sick. Just old."

Annie stared at her hands that she was holding between her dusty knees. "I guess I really understand that, Daddy."

"If you want to, I think Dr. Kurt could find someone with some small children who want a pet more than a riding horse. Someone who would get a kick out of owning a genuine Indian pony . . . and who would give him a good home. Then we could find you a riding horse."

Annie seemed to think that over. From her expression, I knew what the answer would be. "No, Daddy. I looked at the horses that were up for sale at the auction, and none of them was what I wanted. But when we walked out of that tent, and I saw the Chief, I wanted him. Old and bedraggled as he is. He is the horse I wanted."

57

"The Absolutely Perfect Horse," I said.

Annie looked over at me. She wasn't even angry. "Are you very disappointed, Petey?"

A dumb question. Of course I was disappointed. I mean, having a real Indian pony is all right, if he is an Indian pony you can ride and be proud of. But a *retired* Indian pony? I'd rather have had the pinto with the funny front legs. At least he could have been ridden.

"It wasn't my choice," I said.

Dad nodded. "That's right, Petey. Not your choice. If Annie's satisfied, that's all that matters."

"What's Mom going to say? And T.C.?" I asked.

"It's not what Mom is going to say that worries me." Annie ignored anything T.C. might possibly think. "It's what Cathy Thompson is going to spread all over school by Monday morning."

"You're going to be kidded," I said. "You talked too much about the wonderful horse you were going to buy."

"Keep your chin up, my little chickadee," Dad said. "You've taken a big bite. Now it's up to you to chew it."

"Yeah," Annie said. She leaned her face on her arms, which were now stretched out and braced against the dash.

We were out on the main highway now, and Dad's attention was on the road. Annie didn't want to talk anymore, so I stared out the window and wondered what had happened to my only sister. She never used to be a dumb dope. Oh, once in a while she'd do dopey things. What girl didn't? But this was a dumb stunt to top everything crazy she had ever done.

If we had just not gone to the carnival! Was it my fault? I was the one who had wanted to see the side-shows. If we had gone to the auction instead, she might have gotten the gray Arab. Even that fence-chewing bay would have been better than no riding horse at all.

Instead, Annie had let her feelings get mixed up in it, and now she had no horse, but a pet. A liability. She had talked about a companion, but she had bought a patient. Thank goodness, he hadn't cost much . . . though I was afraid the rest of her money might well be spent on vet's fees, trying to get him into shape for riding.

Still, there was something about the old horse. He had carried Indian Maidens down the midway, doing their little act for children, all across the country. Nearly forty years old. Dad was about that age. Forty horse-years equal a hundred and fifty people-years. No wonder he shuffled and dragged his feet when he walked.

Funny, though, how he came to life when Walker put the gear on him and Annie mounted. He perked right up and tried to do his act. There was pride in that . . . he did try. Dad always said the best anybody could do was to try.

The truck slowed, and we turned carefully into the road that led to our farm. "Land ho!" Dad said, as the house came into sight.

"Batten down the hatches . . . shore up all lines!

We're about to hit a squall, mytes. Lubbers below!"
I had a pretty good pirate voice, if I do say so myself.

What it was wasn't exactly a squall. More like the eye of a hurricane. The shocked silence that greeted the Chief when he backed from the trailer with his bony lack of grace, then stood in an attitude of utter weariness, was just what I'd read about, in the center of such a storm. Mom didn't criticize him. The look she gave Dad, though, was something to see.

Annie talked too much, too fast, as she introduced the Chief to Mom and told about buying him away from the dogmeat men. That was a bomb. She should have saved that part for later, when Mom was more used to the sight of him. Everything had to be explained by Dad (and me, too), but no amount of explanation erased the creases from between Mom's eyebrows.

The only unqualified approval the Chief got came from Brad. He liked anything or anyone big. The bigger the better. He always held his arms out to the tallest person around. Though he still crawled rather than walked, he would climb anything that had a handhold. It was a constant task to locate him and get him down from whatever high perch he had climbed to.

When Annie backed the horse from the trailer, Brad came out of the yard as fast as his hands and knees would carry him and planted himself in front of the horse. Then he demanded, with upraised arms and loud squeals, to be picked up. The Chief sniffed at the top of his head with velvety nostrils, making Brad crow with delight. Annie picked the baby up and swung him onto the Chief's back, where he clung, laughing and yelling, as she walked the horse slowly toward his shed.

"Sam," Mom said, when Annie was beyond hearing, "where on earth did she ever see that thing? How could you let her buy that?"

"It's the horse she wanted. For some reason, he's special to her. We'll just have to let her work it out. I could no more have stopped her than I could stop you from doing something you're set on doing. You know how much like you she is."

Mom saw I was listening, so she didn't say anything else. I had the idea that the end of the subject hadn't been explored, as far as she was concerned.

Still, I had a warm feeling from Dad's answer. He didn't know any better than I did why Annie had chosen the horse. I don't think there was a reason. Annie probably couldn't explain it to herself. But the good feeling came when I realized that Dad would go along with her judgment and was willing to let her make her own mistakes, as he would someday allow me to make mine. He would help where he could.

I followed Annie and Brad out to the shed that Dad, T.C., and I had built for the horse. It was built in the old-timey way, out of rough pine logs cut from the young trees we had cleared from our pasture. It was closed to the north, east, and west, open to the south. The roof extended several feet past the closed part of the shed to provide cool shade. Everything

roof was floored deeply with sand and native
⊃m the creek bed, covered over with straw.
norning, someone had sprinkled fresh, sweet-
ferns from the woods and yellow field daisies
all over the straw floor. There were bunches of yellow
brown-eyed Susans in the corners of the feed trough,
which was filled with fresh grain. In the center of
the grain were three carrots, with the tops still on,
standing upright, like birthday candles.

Not someone. Taro Chan. I never knew a boy to
like flowers the way he did. As each new sort of flower
bloomed in the fields and the woods, he came in carrying one carefully selected blossom to show Mom and
to compare with the pictures in the books we had.
He'd even go to the library to find one that we
couldn't identify at home. In the months we had been
on the farm, I guess he had learned more about the
flowers in this part of the country than most of the
natives knew. Latin names, too!

The Chief paid more attention to the flowers than
Annie did. He sniffed at the brown-eyed Susans in
the feed bin, but he decided they weren't as good
to eat as the grain. He buried his nose in that and
began to grind with his jaws.

"I think he's going to have to have bran, or something like that, instead of grain," Annie said. "His
teeth are about gone."

"After you waited such a long time . . . I mean,
you've wanted a horse ever since I can remember . . . why would you pick a toothless old nag?
He really isn't good for anything but dogmeat."

I thought she was going to clobber me with the currycomb. "Don't you say that. Don't ever say that."

"It's true. I mean, he's nice and all that, but you can't ride him with your friends."

"That isn't everything."

"I knew that all along," I said, pushing my luck. "I didn't know you knew it."

Annie went on currying the Chief's mane, a little harder than necessary. The horse didn't seem to mind, though.

"Well, Petey," she said, finally, "I've been thinking about it too. I guess when the time comes to choose, you have to go where your heart goes and forget the plans and the fancy dreams. There was just something about him. I couldn't let him go like that. It just wasn't right."

I took the rough cloth she had for rubbing him down and began to polish the dust off his neck and front quarters. "You sound like something Dad said to us."

"When?" she asked suspiciously.

"When you felt so bad about his bringing Taro Chan home with him."

Annie didn't look at me. She disengaged Brad's grip on the mane close to the saddle-pad, so she could curry that too. Then she was occupied with soothing the baby's indignant wails until she finished and let him grab the mane again.

"I really don't see any connection at all," she said, at last.

"Why don't you like T.C., Annie? He likes you."

63

"Why wouldn't he?" she asked in that sharp tone she always used when T.C. was the subject. "He loves me from the teeth out."

"That's not true!" I was getting angry again. The dust was flying off the Chief's rump in clouds that made me sneeze. It's hard to sound mad while you're sneezing.

Annie caught hold of my shirt and pulled me out into the fresh air. "Here. Breathe for a minute, before you get your allergies all stirred up. Don't tell me you're going to be allergic to horses, too."

"I think it's the dust," I said, between sneezes.

The baby wobbled and almost fell. Annie flew back into the shed and took him down. She brought him outside and set him on top of the rough pine-log fence that ran along the east side of the shelter. She steadied him with one hand, trying to keep his hands out of her hair with the other.

"Petey, Taro Chan is not our real brother. I wish you'd remember that. I know you're crazy about him, and that's O.K. Just don't ask me to be."

"But why, Annie?" I couldn't understand her at all. "He tries so hard. It just isn't like you to dislike anybody."

"If you'd really listen to some of those tales Daddy tells, really listen, you'd know why. He's nothing but an Oriental opportunist. He shifted from one side to the other, until he got into the river patrol and began attaching himself to our naval unit. When he found our daddy, a good soft touch, he dug in like a seed tick."

"That's not fair!" I declared. "Did you ever think how it must be for somebody his age to have lost his family so early he can't remember them? Or how much he must have needed someone to be 'family' for him? Besides, you're twisting things around. And he saved Dad's life."

"His own, too. Remember?"

"Everybody at school likes him," I said, shifting tactics.

"Not everyone," Annie said, her voice grim. "And those that do fawn over him until it makes me sick. He's their token Oriental. An escapee from the Communists. It makes my stomach turn."

"Evan doesn't fawn over anybody," I said. I knew instantly that that wasn't a good example, for she didn't particularly like Evan, either . . . at least, she hadn't before today.

"Evan doesn't have to. Everybody chases after him because he's one of those fractional backs on the football team. I don't know what his motive is for letting Taro Chan hang around him, but I'll bet he's got a motive."

"He helps Evan with his math. Evan helps him with history and English. They're lab partners in science. If they weren't both foreign-born, you wouldn't see a thing wrong with that."

"That's something else. I don't see how Taro Chan could be passing all his courses, unless the teachers are just letting him pass. Since they stopped social promotions here, the girls tell me it's a lot harder school than it used to be."

"And that's not fair, either. That's not even rational. You know T.C. went to school in Thailand. From what Dad tells me, those Catholic schools are tough. He took all kinds of tests before they made out his schedule at school. Dad says he's got a terrific I.Q."

"Dad says." Annie sounded bitter and looked unhappy.

I had a sudden flash of insight. "I don't think you're thinking for yourself, anymore. You don't sound like *you*. I think you're listening to Tanya and that bunch. They're pretty dumb, even for girls. If you ask me, they're a sorry bunch to take for friends."

"I didn't ask you," Annie said with a sniff. "But since you think you know so much, everyone at school is *not* as fond of T.C. as you are."

My temper was getting out of hand. I gave Annie the cloth I'd been using to polish the Chief's rump and took the baby down from the fence rail. I put him under one arm and started for the house.

"Well, you didn't ask me, but I'll tell you, anyway," I threw back over my shoulder. "You don't talk like my sister, anymore. I'm glad you got old Dogmeat, because you can't ride him with that snotty bunch."

I probably would have said more, but the baby squirmed so that I nearly dropped him. I had to put all my attention to getting him right side up and out of the corral gate. By the time I had explained to Mom that I wasn't killing Brad, it wasn't any use to go into the spat with Annie. Being the middle kid is not always easy. Especially when you have been the youngest for a long time.

66

8

While Mom measured tea leaves into the blue-and-gold teapot nobody was allowed to touch but her, I sat behind the table on my bench. I was thinking about the day and counting the knots in the new pine paneling. The new kitchen was nice. Nicer than the one we'd left behind, actually. It was so big.

Before it had become our kitchen, this room had been the parlor of the old house. It had a fireplace on the outside wall, and that was all that remained of the original structure. Dad had the carpenters enclose the part of the front porch that ran in front of the parlor with glass windows. That was where Mom kept her plants. There were also comfortable chairs with bright cushions and a wicker couch painted pale yellow with green cushions. The dining table was arranged so everyone had a good view from the windows. It was pleasant in the winter months to have the greenery inside. And, as now, in spring and summer we could look beyond the growing things to the outside.

From where I sat against the wall, I could see Annie's pasture, the shed, and Annie, still polishing the old horse. From here, he looked just as dusty as he had before, but that could have been a trick of light.

Beyond the table were the work areas Mom had planned for her kitchen. I watched as she took hot rolls from the electric oven, slipped a crusty apple pie into it to warm while we ate. Her motions were quick and economical. She moved around the various work areas in precise patterns.

"I don't suppose you could tell me what made Annie pick that horse," she said, after a bit.

I shook my head. "Dad tried to talk her out of it. I think she felt sorry for it."

"That's logical—but not much reason for getting a thing like that in place of a riding horse. You haven't said much, this afternoon."

"No," I said.

Mom kept on working. When I didn't say anything else, she turned and looked at me. I shrugged. I didn't have anything nice to say. She smiled and turned back to the counter.

"Sam, Junior," she said. "I named you wrong."

T.C. came down the stairs and slid behind the table beside me. "Hey, Petey, how's things?"

68

"Great, T.C. You were so deep in the books I didn't want to bother you."

"That's true," he said. "I have put myself into that history, today. I know more about Sam Houston, now, than I ever wanted to know—but I bet that I'll pass that test on Monday."

"Will you get full credit for the course, if you pass this test?" Mom asked.

"Yes. It's a special thing arranged for me by Mrs. Thompson. She knew I would have to have a credit in Texas history to graduate, so she and Evan and several others have coached me this semester. If I can pass this—*when* I pass this," he corrected himself, "I will get full credit for the year's work. It is good of them, yes?"

"It is good of them, *yes*," Mom affirmed.

"Tell me about Annie's A.P.H., Petey," T.C. said. "Is he exactly what she wanted?"

I shook my head. "Not exactly."

From our bench, we could see her come from the shed, the old horse walking with her, his head draped over her shoulder. When she closed the gate behind her, he pressed against it, then hung his head over and nickered after her. He looked as if he expected to come into the house with her.

"Looks as if you made a fast conquest." Mom smiled at Annie as she came into the kitchen.

Annie looked at me uneasily. But when she saw everyone was easy and relaxed, she knew I had said nothing about our fuss. She smiled at me apologetically.

"Looks like it, Mom. I guess he's always had lots of things going on around him. He feels lonesome out here."

"He hasn't had time to get lonesome yet," Dad said, coming into the kitchen.

"When he fattens up some, he really will be beautiful. He has such pretty markings."

"But he's really awful-looking now," I said to her. She made a face at me . . . but not a mad face.

"I don't believe that Annie would choose an awful-looking horse," T.C. said in his softly accented voice. He was smiling at her across the table.

Annie got that hooded look on her face, even though she smiled back. "You have to come out after supper and see for yourself, Taro Chan."

"Yes. I want to. I have had enough of studying old things for a while."

I couldn't help laughing out loud. Annie got very red in the face, and T.C. looked from one to the other of us and finally at Dad, completely puzzled. Dad was suspiciously near to grinning, too.

"I don't know what I said that was funny," T.C. said.

"Well, the horse is rather old," Dad said. "Still, Annie's going to have to get used to that and not be sensitive about it."

"I'm beginning to realize that." She sounded sad. "Petey, lay off the sniggers, will you?"

T.C. kicked me hard under the table. "I did not intend any reference to your horse, Annie," he said.

70

"I was talking about the history. If I pass this test Monday, I have a credit made."

Outside, the old horse nickered again and rattled the gate.

"I'll tell you who has it made." Dad winked at Annie. "A retirement home and a personal hand-maiden to attend his every whim."

"Don't eat so fast, " Mom cautioned Annie. "He isn't going anywhere."

"Did Petey tell you that your evzone friend came to Annie's rescue this morning?"

"Evzone! Evzone! He's no warrior. Just an arrogant Greek chauvinist. He thinks every girl in school is chasing him," Annie said with unnecessary heat.

"He looked like a warrior to me this afternoon even if he had on jeans instead of one of those white pleated tutus. How could they fight in those things?" I asked Dad.

He shrugged. "Different times, Petey. I guess the puffy sleeves and pleated skirts all had a purpose at one time. Now, it's just a costume, like gyrene blues."

"Or Navy whites," Mom said.

"I've seen a lot of red stuff on some of those Navy whites. Makes it hard for me to think of them as a costume," Dad said.

T.C., who had been silent, said, "I think I am not following this conversation very well. I have been deep in my books all day. Was there a fight? Tell me. Evan came to your rescue? How?" His dark eyes

71

flicked between Dad and Annie as they told him the events of that morning.

"He is a good person," T.C. said, when they finished. "I do not think I'd like to fight with him."

"Looked to me as if he'd have enjoyed tangling with those guys from the truck," I said. "Do you always pick tigers for friends?"

"It is the tigers who survive." T.C.'s voice was sober, even though he smiled.

"You looked like you wouldn't have minded, either," I reminded Dad.

Dad laughed silently, widely, in a way that made his ears flatten against his head.

Mom looked at him with her chilled-ice glance. "I didn't send you off this morning to get into a brawl."

"It wasn't a real brawl, Mom," Annie said soothingly. "Just a little misunderstanding about who bought the horse. Evan did delay them until Dad arrived."

"Well," Mom said, still unsatisfied, "I can't imagine fighting over that poor old thing."

Spots of color showed in Annie's cheeks. Dad shifted the talk slightly. "Annie, why don't you introduce T.C. to your horse before you do the dishes. Then he can help Petey with the little calves before it gets dark."

The supper dishes were always Annie's, but I usually helped with them. Today, I didn't think I'd offer to.

The old horse nickered when he saw Annie coming outside. When she opened the gate, he pushed his head against her, making funny little noises as if he were greeting her.

"It does not seem possible he would know you so soon," T.C. said.

The old horse turned to him and sniffed his chest, blowing through his nostrils in noisy whuffles.

"Why is he doing this?" T.C. said uneasily. He had no experience with horses.

"He's just getting acquainted," Annie said. "He does that with everyone he meets."

"He will know me the next time?" T.C. cautiously patted the Chief lightly on the wide part of his jaw.

"I expect he will. Here . . . do this." Annie showed him how to scratch under the throat and between the jaws. The old horse sighed and closed his eyes, leaning his head against T.C.'s chest.

"He does have nice markings, Annie. Though I was expecting a horse with white stockings," T.C. said, continuing to scratch.

"The A.P.H.? No, he isn't that, is he?" She laughed. "Funny, though, how he seemed to know me when I walked up to him. He came right over. I wanted him as soon as I saw him. He wasn't like anything I had pictured, but I wanted him, anyway." Unsmiling, she said, "Mom keeps wanting a reason that I picked him. I don't have anything I can pin down. Do people have to have reasons for everything they do?"

"I stopped looking for reasons, even for logic, a long time ago," T.C. answered. "Things will happen as they will, even though science always looks for reasons. Perhaps it is the spirits who direct our lives, as my people believe."

"You believe in spirits, T.C.? Like ghosts?" Annie frowned.

"Of course. For everything, there is a spirit that does not die. Is it not so in your religion?"

"Whoa. I don't want to get into a religious discussion, the way you and Daddy do. I do believe in people's souls. Tree spirits . . . rock spirits . . . animal spirits . . . I don't know about that. I read somewhere that spirits of the dead stay with us and guide us. It gives me a creepy feeling to think about it."

"Only if the spirits are bad do we need to be afraid," T.C. said.

"Yeah," I put in. "But how do you tell the good ones from the bad ones?"

"Ah." T.C. backed away from the horse and put a hand on my shoulder. "It is with the spirits as it is with the living. We take what we see and hope for the best. The spirits who directed Annie to her horse were good spirits, I think."

"Good for old Dogmeat, anyway," I said. "Come on, before it gets dark, we have to take feed down to the calves."

We turned to go, but Annie stopped us. "Thanks for the flowers, T.C. That was you, wasn't it?"

He smiled at her over his shoulder. "Perhaps it was the spirits."

9

The seven Angus calves were Dad's pride. They were also T.C.'s responsibility . . . and mine. We hadn't had them long. Two months or so, and already they had developed personalities as individual as those of people. The little bull was already feeling his responsibilities and his importance as the future father of our herd. He was the first one to taste whatever food was put out for his group. Also the first to greet anyone who come into his pasture. His name was MacTavish, Mac for short. The heifers were Anise, Licorice, Chocolate, Brownie, Coco, and Tar Baby.

They were kept away from the larger herd of Herefords in a small pasture we called the Gopher Field (for obvious reasons). It had raised a great crop of gophers every year since Mom could remember. Now we had greater ambitions for it. We'd spent a lot of time trapping the little rodents down to a reasonable population. We'd harrowed the field, smoothing out their mounded burrows, and now it was even and covered with grass. To get to the Gopher Field, we drove the tractor through the front pasture, across the shallow creek, and up a steep bank. I drove, T.C. standing behind on the drawbar and hanging on to the seat.

The calves weren't hard to find. Although there were thick woods to hide in, they knew the sound of the tractor . . . and that that sound meant feed pellets. There were six shadowy figures standing at the wire gap when we drove up. Mac was slightly apart from the girls. He knew where the food would be put down. T.C. had to shoo the heifers back when he opened the gap, so I could drive in.

We kicked hay off the little trailer in a short line, so each calf would have room to eat without interference from its neighbor. Alongside the hay, we dropped a line of hard pellets. In spite of our precautions, there were several head buttings over choice piles of hay before they finally settled down to eat. While they ate, we rubbed their backs and talked to them, to get them used to the sounds of our voices and to being handled. Someday, they might be show-class calves. Their blood was certainly good enough.

"You really like it here, don't you?" I asked T.C., after watching him run his fingers through the black

curls of the little bull's back. He was crooning something in Vietnamese, I suppose it was, to the critter.

"Of course I do. Why would I not?"

I shrugged. "I don't know. Sometimes I try to think
what it would be like to leave Dad and Mom and
go to live somewhere where nobody spoke my language and everyone looked a bit different from me."

"Petey, it's funny. I forget I don't look just like
everybody else. And English has been my main language since I was about ten. It comes naturally, now,
though I still have trouble keeping up with the slang
words."

"But don't you miss your parents?" I persisted. It
was something that had worried me for a long time.

"I think about them, sometimes, what tiny bit I
can remember. But that is so little! Your father is
my father, now, and this is my home. You are my
brother. I suppose I want to forget that other place.
I have a lot of things to forget."

"Like your real name? Dad said you were too little
even to know that, when you were found, but I'd
think you might get a hint of it, sometimes."

"I remember a name. I'm not sure it was even mine.
It could have been a name I heard somewhere later.
Anyway, it wasn't important to me, anymore. Sister
Toyoko had already started calling me Taro Chan,
and after a while everyone called me that. It was as
good a name as any."

"Isn't Chan a Chinese name, as in Charlie Chan?"
I asked. "Why don't you take an American name?"

T.C. shrugged. "I don't know if it's Chinese, or care. It's American now, like T.C. T.C. Braeden is a pretty good American name. As you have reminded me, I do have an Oriental face. Better to have an Oriental name. Most Americans wouldn't know a Japanese name from a Chinese or any other Far Eastern one, anyway. Unless they served in Korea or 'Nam." He slapped the little bull on the rump so hard that it jumped and trotted away a few steps. It looked around at him reproachfully, before returning to eat more pellets. "I'm glad to be here, to have a mother and father. I like going to school, and I enjoy my friends there. You've been great. I only wish . . ." He didn't finish, and I knew what he was thinking.

"Annie?"

He nodded.

"I don't know what's wrong with her," I said. I think I must have sounded as disgusted as I felt. "I think it's that bunch she hangs out with at school. They're a gang of snobs."

"Tanya!" T.C. shook his head. "Evan likes Annie. She is friendly enough with me, but I have the feeling sometimes that she doesn't mean it. Like tonight. Annie showed me her horse very politely, but I had the feeling she would rather not."

"Dumb girls!" My teeth were clenched.

"Not just girls. There are some boys, too . . . but I do not expect everyone to be my friend. Nor do I really want that. It does not matter. But I do care whether Annie likes me. I wish it could be more than an armed truce with her."

78

"She'll come around," I said, wondering if she would. "Just ignore her."

"I've been trying that for a year. Still, there is not much else I can do, is there?" He shoved a couple of heifers out of his way. "Come. Let's walk the fence to check for loose wire and posts. I told Sam we would do that this week."

I followed him as he pulled on the posts, testing and checking for loose staples along the wire. We found where the calves had pushed a post until it wobbled in its hole and would need to be reset. On the creek side, where the fence was a part of the old original fencing, the wire was rusted and loose in two places. I used a piece of white rag from under the seat of the tractor to tie on, marking the spots that needed repairing.

A rustle at my feet made me jump. I saw the glistening hump of an armadillo, followed closely by four smaller shapes. They moved like clockwork toys, and you almost expected to hear a *click-click-click* as their tiny legs worked.

"Armadillo," T.C. said. He laughed. "Do you know what I read about them? They always have exactly four babies, no more, no less. And the four are always either boys or girls, never mixed. Very odd."

"Are they good to eat?"

"Bobcats love them. I read that people used to eat them, too. I'd have to be very hungry to try one, though."

The south end of the Gopher Field ran into the trees of our Deep Woods. About a hundred acres was part of the timber forest owned by a big timber company. It butted up against ours, and we were glad they used selective cutting and kept their woods wild. In the fall, they allowed hunters to come into their woods to hunt for squirrel and deer. Sometimes the deer came into the pasture with the Herefords or the Angus calves to browse. And sometimes they jumped into the hayfields. We didn't want them there. Dad always clapped his hands loudly and chased them out, knowing that they'd be back later. Still, he didn't hunt or allow hunters on our timberland. When he posted the land, he said, "I've had enough of killing. I would rather have live animals around."

Once, T.C. and I had seen a bobcat by the creek . . . only for a moment. As soon as he heard us, he turned and flashed his round golden eyes in our direction. Then he slipped, ghostlike, into the shadows and disappeared.

"Like the tiger." T.C. had laughed. "You can stand next to a tiger in the forest, and you won't know he is there until he opens his eyes and looks at you. Of course," he added, "sometimes you do not see his eyes until he has you by the leg."

"Did you ever see a real tiger? I mean loose? In the forest?"

"Twice. Fortunately, both times they were frightened by gunfire and were moving away when I saw them. They came after the battles sometimes and dragged bodies away, they tell me. It is easier than hunting in a forest where most of the game has been killed or driven off. There were many people in Thailand who, like me, had been forced out of Vietnam. They told tales that would curl your hair."

"That's terrible," I said.

T.C. shook his head. "No. I don't think so. We have ruined and destroyed so much of their hunting ground, all over Vietnam and Cambodia. There is, in everything, the wish to live. First it was the tiger's jungle. I do not think it is terrible . . . it does not matter to the dead man, and the tiger needs food, just as we do."

"That's a strange way to look at things."

"Different. Not necessarily wrong."

I had to agree with that, but I filed the conversation away to ask Dad about, when I had a chance.

I was thinking about bobcats and armadillos and tigers when T.C., who was driving the tractor back to the house, stopped. "Listen!" he said.

From the darkness of the woods at the lower end of our pasture came the sound of a pack of dogs on the hunt. Hounds belled through the woods, after some small creature. They were probably deer dogs. It wasn't illegal in our county to hunt with packs of dogs. Many people, like Mr. Blackburn, whom we had met that morning at the auction, raised and trained dogs to hunt, chasing the deer out of cover so the hunters could shoot them. It didn't seem very sporting to me, even though there was something exciting about hearing the dogs as they yelled, unseen, after their quarry.

I had my arms around T.C.'s waist, and I felt him shudder. "I do not care for hunters," he said. "Two legged or four legged."

We listened until the dog pack faded into the woods. Then we started up the tractor and went home.

10

Light spring rain fell through the night and into the next morning, just hard enough to make everyone want to turn over and go back to sleep. I heard Dad get up early. Then I heard the tractor. He had gone to feed the Herefords. Mom was teasing him about being an otter. All those years in the underwater demolition team had made him impervious to rain. And it was true. He didn't seem to mind getting wet at all.

Annie did. She hated to get wet, but in spite of that, I heard her slip from her room and out the door. Going to check on her horse, I guessed. She didn't try to ride him until much later in the day.

T.C. didn't come home after church. Instead, he stayed in town to have lunch with Evan. They planned to go over that history one more time before the big test tomorrow. I read until my eyes started to water, then I wandered out looking for Annie. She was tightening the blanket saddle around the Chief's back. The sun was coming out.

"I didn't think you were going to ride him," I said, rubbing his nose.

"I didn't think it would hurt to try him out, just to see what he can do. He might not be so bad," she said.

Annie mounted easily from the fence, sliding onto his back so lightly that he didn't seem to notice. As before, he seemed to straighten up once she was on his back, pointing his ears sharply forward and pulling in his lower lip so it didn't hang down. With his head up and his chin tucked back, he stepped out in an elegant parade walk, his knees springing high, his hooves snapping out smartly. There was a loud clicking sound when his weight shifted from ankle to ankle, but I didn't laugh. He was trying.

Annie rode out the gate and out of sight down the curving drive. From where I stood, I could see the Chief's sides start to heave before they disappeared.

The barn cat brought her kittens out into the afternoon sunshine, and I played with them for a while, waiting for Annie to come back. When she didn't, I began to worry.

A pickup turned into our road and stopped beside

me. "Hi, Petey. Where's your dad?" Dr. Kurt stepped out of the truck and stretched.

For a big man, he was graceful. He looked big enough to handle a full-grown steer, which he had done in his rodeo days in college. Yet now, when he picked up the calico kitten I'd been playing with, she didn't seem at all out of place in his big hands. I guess that's what made him a good vet.

"He's in the house. I'll go get him."

But there was no need. Dad had heard the pickup drive up and came onto the porch. "Hey! Have time for coffee?"

Dr. Kurt handed me the kitten and walked toward the house. "Sorry, not this time. I came to get the trailer. Have to pick up some calves to make some lab tests. Come with me, won't you?"

"I'd like to," Dad said. "Wait a minute." He went into the house while I helped Dr. Kurt unhitch the trailer from our pickup and attach it to his.

When Dad came out, he had on a clean shirt. His chin was smooth, and a trace of powder remained where he had quickly run the razor over his face. He smelled fresh and limey. It would be a long time before I could shave, but I liked to splash on some of that lime-scented shaving lotion once in a while, anyway. Maybe it might make the whiskers grow faster!

"Where's Annie?" Dad asked, looking at the open gate. He turned to Dr. Kurt before I could answer. "I'd like you to see the horse she picked. You won't believe it."

85

"Did she find that perfect horse?"

"Not exactly," Dad answered. "I want to see what you think."

"*I* think she's a nut," I said. "She went riding a long time ago. Ought to be back soon."

"Riding?" Dad looked at me with an odd expression and turned back to Dr. Kurt. "Well, you can look him over when you bring me back. Want to go along, Petey?"

I didn't. If T.C. didn't return soon, I would have to feed the calves by myself, but before I got around to that I wanted to see what was keeping Annie.

When the trailer bounced out of sight, I got my bike from the barn and pedaled after Annie, following her horse's hoof marks in the damp sand of the road. The track was easy to follow. When she had reached the hard-surfaced road outside our gate, she had turned toward the woodlands, riding along the wide shoulder of the road. The Chief needed to be reshod, and the hardtop would have hurt his feet. By the time the tracks reached our fence line, there were long scuff marks for each front hoofprint. Not quite a mile, and he was too tired to pick up his feet.

At the wooden bridge, which crossed the spring-fed creek in which we sometimes swam and fished for bream, the tracks led off the road. I knew I would find them at the clearing, where the creek ran shallow over clean white sand. There the pines made a kind of umbrella of shade over everything. The rain had cleaned the air, making all the scents of the woods stand out sharply. Rain, too, put the birds to drying

86

their feathers busily. Many were hunting insects that were out drying their wings. Wet bushes slapped me as I turned off the road and into the clearing.

The Chief stood in the creek, in water up to his ankles. Annie knelt in the water and splashed it up on his legs, rubbing them. He reached down and snuffled the back of her neck. I could hear her talking to him.

"Hey!" I called. "What are you doing?"

Annie straightened, not as glad to see me as the Chief was. He nickered a greeting. "I'm giving him a rubdown," Annie said. "What does it look like?"

I shrugged, dropped my bike, and found a reasonably dry spot to sit upon on the creek bank. "How does he ride?"

"Very slowly." Annie shook her head. "He started to shake about the time I hit the road at the gate. I rode this far, but he's all done in. He's just never going to be a riding horse, Petey."

"What good is a horse you can't ride?"

"Pete," Annie said, very sharply. Then she stopped. Instead, she shook her head again and said, "If I knew that, I'd try to explain it to you. It's just one of those things. Like they say in the cowboy movies, a person does what he has to do."

That didn't make any more sense than buying the old horse in the first place. I changed the subject. "Dr. Kurt came by for the trailer. He wants to see your horse when he brings Dad back, after a while."

Annie frowned. I guess she knew what he'd say. We goofed around there a bit longer, but I knew

I had to get home to tend the calves. Annie came with me. When we reached the road, the old horse Annie was leading stopped as if he expected to be mounted.

"Come on. I need the exercise more than you do," Annie said, walking on for a few steps.

He looked puzzled and finally shook his head before stepping out and catching up with her. He put his head over her shoulder, and she rubbed his nose, talking softly to him as we walked home together, me pushing my bike. It didn't seem right to ride, when she had to walk.

T.C. wasn't home yet, so Annie helped me load the feed for the calves. Then she went inside to help Mom with dinner, while I took the feed to the Gopher Field. The calves weren't at the fence to meet me. Even when I drove the tractor into the pasture, they didn't run up as they usually did but huddled nervously at the edge of the trees. They didn't seem to know me, after all the times I'd fed them. I had to walk after them, driving them in circles, edging them close enough to the hay and pellets until the food was practically under their noses. It was terribly different. Always, they'd been eager, seeming glad not only to get the feed but to see T.C. and me.

I couldn't see anything wrong with them. Once they realized that I was me and I'd brought feed, they huddled close to me, each one wanting to be stroked and talked to. Even Mac pushed close for his rubbing. They stopped feeding to follow me to the gate as I drove the tractor out. They must have been playing awfully hard, I thought, for the ground was cut up all along the fence from the actions of their sharp little hooves.

Dr. Kurt and Dad were back when I got to the house. I joined them in the Chief's pasture. I was curious about what Dr. Kurt had to say about the old horse.

He was bent over, touching some little white spots on the Chief's front legs. He called them cannon bones and said they were "firing marks," which showed the horse had sometime or other bowed those tendons. It was a kind of injury that happened to racehorses most often, but also it could happen to horses whose work required them to start and stop fast. Like rodeo horses.

"He probably had some careless handling, away back there," Dr. Kurt said.

Before he gave his verdict, he folded the eyelids back, studying each eye carefully. He pinched the lower lip gently to study the stubs of teeth.

"Annie," he said at last, "I think he has been a good horse at one time. A very good horse. He's an Appaloosa, probably a real reservation Appaloosa. It still shows in his lines. But he's done a fair amount of work in the past, and now he's ready to go out to pasture. He'll never be a riding horse again. Not what you've wanted and talked about for so long."

Annie didn't look at anybody, just kept rubbing the Chief's shoulder and sort of leaning against it. "I know, Dr. Kurt. I guess I knew that yesterday."

"Then, why?"

She shrugged. "I liked him. He liked me. I couldn't let them take him for dogmeat. I just couldn't."

Dr. Kurt looked over the Chief's back at Dad. I knew they'd made some kind of arrangement.

"No, I don't like the idea of the dogmeat men myself. Tell you what, Annie. I have a nice big pasture on my farm with fourteen good horses on it. One more won't make a bit of difference. Why don't you let me take him over to my place? You can bring my little sorrel filly, Dancer, over here and ride her. I may be able to put a bit of meat on the Chief and get him in riding condition, before the summer is over."

Dancer! Wow! I wouldn't give you a nickel for most of the horses in the county, but I'd seen that filly. She was the prettiest thing I ever saw. She was a tall horse, slim, with one long white stocking and three white socks and a snip of white in the middle of her nose. She had a long, light-golden mane, which floated when she trotted across the field, which she always did when anyone drove past her pasture. Dancer for old Dogmeat . . . Annie would have to be crazy not to take a trade like that.

The Chief wasn't used to long silences from Annie. He seemed uneasy, too, because of Dr. Kurt's probing attention. He pushed at Annie with his nose and whuffed his breath softly against her shoulder. Annie rubbed him gently. Then she smiled at Dr. Kurt, the way she does when her mind is made up.

"Thanks, Dr. Kurt. I really would like to ride Dancer sometime. But I don't think the old Chief would like being left by himself with just a bunch of horses. He hasn't been around horses in years. He likes people. I think he feels good, being with me. I do wish you'd tell me what to feed him, though."

"Annie"—Dad's voice held a bit of hopelessness—"I think perhaps you might wait a little before you decide. Kurt's offer is a generous one. You've wanted a good horse for so long . . . a riding horse."

The set expression on her face didn't change. Her voice said, "I'll think about it," but her face didn't agree. I knew she had already decided. She was going to keep the Chief.

While everyone was talking, Mom came out of the house, the baby toddling along beside her, hanging on to her hand. When he was close enough, he turned loose and got down to business on his hands and knees, rushing over to Annie. She caught him and swung him to her shoulder. He leaned over and grabbed the Chief's mane with both hands. Annie had to pull hard to loosen his grip.

The Chief turned his neck and sniffed loudly at the baby. Brad squealed and started on one of his foreign-language conversations. The old horse nodded wisely, as if in answer to the baby's questions. Everyone laughed.

"You may not have a riding horse, but he's going to make a first-class baby-sitter," Dr. Kurt said.

"I do believe he's laughing, too," Mom said, patting the Chief's neck.

I was standing directly in front of the horse, and I thought he winked. Blinked, of course. Horses don't wink. He did look contented, though, like a cat looks when she's purring. Horses don't purr, either. They just switch their tails and look as if they have the world and a dozen apples.

You dumb old horse, I said silently. *You old dogmeat, you. You ought to look contented. Here you've bewitched Annie and wrapped her around your pin-fired cannon bones. Good food to eat, a pasture of your own, no work. An old con horse, you are.*

I glared at the horse, who didn't notice. Then I stomped back toward the house. I didn't understand Annie at all anymore. Worse than that, here were our perfectly sensible parents, who let her act like a dumb girl! I bet myself they would never let me pull a stunt like buying that useless horse.

Wait until I was ready to buy my motorcycle! Not that I would buy a crock, as Annie had done, but they'd never allow me to do anything that dumb!

11

The phone rang just as I stepped up on the porch. It was for Dr. Kurt. Mom and Dad had moved slowly toward the house, and they met him at his truck as he bounded back out of the house, rumpling my hair as he passed me. I'm going to shave my head. It won't be stylish, but it will stop people from messing with it.

"Sam, you heard any dogs around here?" Dr. Kurt asked.

Dad shook his head. "Not near. We hear dogs, sometimes, in the woods. Hunting. Haven't noticed anything special. Why?"

"That was Tom Laney, just down the road from you. Wants me to come right over. He had a couple of calves savaged by wolves or by dogs. I'd put my money on dogs. Aren't enough wolves . . . and besides, they seldom attack big, healthy stock. Dogs will, though, just for the fun of it."

"T.C. and I heard a pack of hounds in the woods last night," I said.

"When? Where were you?" Dr. Kurt looked worried.

"When we went out to feed the Angus calves. They weren't really close. We listened for a while, but they went out of hearing without coming near us."

"The Angus are still over in that west field?" Dr. Kurt looked at Dad, who nodded. "That's pretty far away. If there are wolves or a pack of wild dogs out there, you might better bring them up to a closer pasture, near the house."

Dad nodded again. "Good idea. I'll cut that small pasture east of the house in the morning and tighten up the fence. The boys can help me bring them up when they get home from school."

Dr. Kurt agreed. "The Herefords are big enough to take care of themselves, especially with the big range bull you have. I'd keep the Angus up close, until we know what happened to Laney's calves."

When he had gone, Dad questioned me about the dogs we had heard. Finally, he said, "I want you boys to be careful in the woods. If there is a pack of wolves around, they won't bother you a bit. You'll never see them. But dogs are different. They are used to people—not afraid of them at all. They're used to livestock, too. They'll attack people, if they're mean enough and wild enough. If you hear them, get on the tractor and come right home."

"I didn't hear them tonight when I was down there."

"That's another thing, Petey. When T.C. is off with Evan, you wait for me to go with you. I don't want either of you boys going down there by yourselves for a while. Buddy up, O.K.?"

"Can we take the twenty-two when we go to feed the calves?"

T.C. was an expert shot, as Dad was. Neither of them had ever seemed willing to teach me. Maybe now was the time.

Dad didn't smile. "I don't think it's necessary, yet. I don't want you shooting up the place before we're sure the enemy is out there. Let's don't pop off any friendlies."

"Everybody in school knows how to shoot, except for me. They shoot at cans and stuff."

"Yeah," Dad said. "Stuff like insulators on telephone poles and road signs and songbirds. You'll learn soon enough about guns, Petey. Don't rush it."

T.C. came home after I had gone to sleep. I didn't see him at all until morning. After breakfast, the three of us walked down the curving road to the bus stop to wait for the yellow school bus. It was seldom that we had to wait more than five minutes for it. It would wait up to five minutes for us, if we weren't there when it stopped for us.

The bus was seldom more than half full when it came to our stop, so we always had a good seat going

95

in. Coming home was different. In the afternoon, the driver allowed the first and second graders (six or seven of them) to get on first and to sit close to him, up front. Everyone else had to take their chances on a seat, so I usually stood most of the way. I really didn't mind. It was kind of fun to hang on to the polished rail and sway with the motion of the bus. Of course, I was forced to gripe about it, or everybody would think there was something wrong with me.

None of Annie's friends rode our bus. Most of them lived in town, and they really looked down, more than a little, on the "country kids" who had to ride a bus, instead of being brought in their parents' cars (or driving their own!). So Annie usually sat with Brenda Marshall, who was on the large side. Annie is almost the only person, except for the little kids, who is skinny enough to fit on a seat with her comfortably.

Brenda had a pretty face and nice hair—kind of goldy-red and wavy. She let it hang down in waves and pinned it back with a gold-colored clip or tied it with a ribbon. It always looked nice, and she did too, fat or not. Her dresses and shirts were always crisp and clean, and she smelled nice.

The Marshall farm was a dairy, and Brenda had a collie dog with some pups. She was more friendly than Annie's other school friends, and I guess that was why I liked her more. She asked Annie to come over to see her nearly every day . . . and told her to bring me, so I could play with the pups! I think she'd have given me one, if Dad would have let me keep it.

This morning, Brenda was full of questions about the horse Annie had bought. I suppose everyone in school had heard about the A.P.H. and that she was finally going to get it. Brenda didn't seem to know about the rumble at the fair, because her questions were all about how he looked and how he rode. She had never had a horse and didn't seem to want one. She was sensible, as well as friendly.

Annie spent a lot of time describing the Chief as he had probably looked years ago. She went into detail about what Mr. Walker had told us about his rodeo background. She even said some things that I didn't remember, which is not like Annie at all. If Brenda ever came over to the house to see that horse, she was going to wonder what had happened to him. I poked T.C. in the ribs, but he frowned at me and looked straight ahead. So I sat still and listened.

Annie's bunch were waiting at the bus stop when we arrived at school. They surrounded her quickly, leaving Brenda outside their circle, as they always did. It made me sort of mad. T.C. stood back with me, listening to their talk. His face wasn't happy.

Ross Blackburn wasn't even willing to wait for the preliminary hellos to be said. "How's old Dogmeat?" he asked.

"If you mean the Chief, he's fine." One thing about Annie . . . she could always play things really cool.

"Oh, I think Dogmeat's a much better name for

him. It's so original," Cathy simpered.

Evan, who had pulled into the parking lot in his red jeep, parked and walked over to T.C. and me. Now he pushed his way into the group beside Annie. "There's probably a better name for you, too, Cathy," he said coldly. "I don't think you'd like to be called by it."

Cathy sputtered, and the group laughed. "Well, you saw the old thing. You nearly had to fight to save him from the dogmeat men. What would you call him?"

I saw Annie put her hand on Evan's arm to keep him from saying anything more.

"I don't care what you call him, Cathy. Petey calls him Dogmeat. But he's my horse, and I'll call him whatever I want to. Maybe Dogmeat would be a good name. It will remind me of what would have happened if I hadn't come along."

"If you hadn't come along," Tanya said, "you'd have gone to the auction and bought a real horse. Now how are you going to ride with us?"

"I can, when I want to," Annie said. "Dr. Kurt said I could ride Dancer whenever I like."

"It's not the same as having your own horse, though," Tanya insisted.

Ross laughed. "Well, when you get tired of nursing old Dogmeat, my dad can always use him."

Annie looked at him blankly.

"We've got eight deer hounds. We can always use a little more dogmeat." Ross laughed again, with an edge to his voice.

Evan's face became quite red. Annie's was pale. T.C. began moving into the group, and I started away, looking for a teacher. The bell rang, thank goodness, and the group began to break up. The last I saw of Annie, Evan was walking on one side of her and T.C. on the other. She was walking a bit jerkily, and she seemed to be as angry as I ever remember seeing her.

When we met at the bus that afternoon, Annie looked tired and on the edge of tears.

"You O.K.?" I asked.

She looked at me a minute before answering. "Sure, Petey. Hard day."

"That bunch tease you all day?" I clenched my fists, knowing there wasn't a thing I could do about it if they had.

"They were pretty mean. Even Tanya. It would have been worse, I think, but every time I turned around either Evan or T.C. was there. It was a bit like learning a new word—every time you turn around there it is in a book or a magazine. I never paid much attention to Evan before today, but he was everywhere I went."

"Who was?" T.C. asked from behind her. Annie turned around quickly and stepped back.

"Whoops, careful! You'll step on something important—me!" Evan said.

"Are you following me around?"

"What do you think?" Evan asked, grinning.

"I think I'm glad," Annie said, holding out her hand. Her "Thanks!" included both of them.

The little kids were on the bus and seated. The driver opened the doors to the mob. I hung back. No use getting caught in the crush.

Annie started for the door, but Evan stopped her. "Why don't you all ride with me today? If you're not in a hurry to get home, that is. I have to stop for gas."

I stopped in my tracks. Evan had driven T.C. and me home a lot of times, and I loved to ride in the jeep. Annie never had.

"If you don't mind," T.C. said, "I must get on home. The bus will arrive before you, my friend. Come on, Petey. We have to help Sam with the little calves."

I started to get on the bus, but Annie stopped me. "It's out of your way, Evan."

"About five miles, and it's a lovely day for a ride," Evan answered.

"If you really don't mind, I don't want to ride the bus today. I've had just about enough of people. We'd like to ride with you."

Annie didn't look at me, but she gave me a little push toward the jeep. She wasn't smiling.

"Take your time," T.C. said from the doorway of the bus. "I will tell everyone where you are. It will be O.K." He gave me some kind of signal that didn't register then, and I saw him explaining to the driver that Annie and I would be driving home with Evan. The driver nodded. He knew that T.C. and I rode with Evan at times, and that it was all right with Dad.

Evan handed Annie into the jeep elegantly, while I hopped over the back and sat on one of the boxes behind the seats. He was proud of this jeep, and it showed. He had painted it himself, a bright red. His mother had helped him re-cover the seats and carpet the floor with scraps of colorful carpeting. Evan kept the jeep shining clean. On Saturdays, he used it to make deliveries for his father's grocery store.

"Sorry there's no top," he said, reaching across Annie to the tiny glove compartment. "Here's a scarf my mother keeps to use when she rides with me. If you want your hair to stay on, that is."

"Oh, good!" Annie said and smiled at him. It was an odd smile. Not quite real.

Evan shook his head. "Rough day, huh?"

Annie nodded, her lower lip quivering.

He kicked the engine over and raced it a couple of times. "Noisy," he said loudly, leaning toward her. "We'll have to talk later." Then he looked back at me. "Hang on, podner!" he said, his eyes twinkling. We started off with a roar and a jump.

It was smart of him not to talk to Annie just yet. She was about to bawl, but I didn't know exactly why. Unless somebody at school had said something else about old Dogmeat.

In spite of the wheel-squealing start at school, Evan drove very carefully through town, staying well within the speed limits and obeying the stop signs and traffic lights.

"I pay for my own mistakes," he had explained

to T.C. once, when taking us home.

"How many tickets have you paid?" I had asked him.

"Not a one, yet. And I don't intend to pay any, either. I work hard for my money. I'm not going to throw it away on something I can avoid." He stopped for the third stop sign in a four-block area and added, through clenched teeth, "Even if the laws are stupid."

Evan had let me drive the jeep from the hard-surfaced road up to the house. It wasn't a long way, but it was long enough to give me a feel of the jeep. It wasn't any harder to drive than the tractor, at least at a slow speed. But I doubted that he'd let me drive today, with Annie along.

Evan pulled the jeep into a service station and had the tank filled. The attendant was busy filling other cars, so he checked his own radiator and tires while I sat in the jeep with Annie. I tried to make conversation, but she gave such short answers that I gave up and sat back.

Annie wasn't in a good mood. I thought she was crying, once, but she didn't sniff or rub away tears. Evan didn't say anything to either of us, though he looked at Annie out of the corner of his eye several times. I thought from the set of his mouth that he was angry about something.

Without asking if we wanted them or not, he stopped at a drive-in for drinks. It was one of those places that serve root beers in big frosted mugs, which is my favorite way of drinking them. It is a self-service place. Naturally, I was elected to go and get the drinks.

Service took a while, because it's just about every-body's favorite after-school place. When I carried the mugs back to the jeep, Annie looked as if she were really going to cry. Evan looked madder than ever. He was talking in a low tone to her. She would just nod, without answering. Whatever he was saying didn't seem to be helping much.

"Petey, go tell Chaney that I'm taking you two home. We'd like to take the mugs with us. I'll return them when I get back to town."

I didn't know Chaney, the guy who ran the root beer place, except by sight. I figured that Evan did. When I told him, he looked out at Evan, who waved back.

"Sure, kid," Chaney said. He lifted his hand to wave O.K. at Evan.

Riding with the drinks in the open jeep made the frosting melt off them too fast, but it was better than no drinks at all. The five miles out to the farm seemed very short. Too short. When Evan slowed to turn into our drive, Annie touched him on the arm and pointed down the road toward the bridge. "Can you drive down there first?"

"Sure," he said. "I want a chance to finish our con-versation."

He turned off the road into the little grove by the creek, at Annie's direction. He stopped under the pines. "It's pretty down here," Evan said. He cut the motor, and the silence under the pines surrounded us.

"I like to come down here," Annie said, getting

out of the jeep and kneeling on the sandy bank of the creek. She splashed the cold water on her face, getting her hair wet on the ends.

Evan climbed out and leaned against the front of the jeep, watching Annie. I scrunched down in the back and wished I had made them let me out at our road. It was still not too far to walk home, if they fooled around too long. I had to help with the calves before dark.

"Evan," Annie asked, a questioning note in her voice, "you really seem to like Taro Chan. Why?"

He laughed, startled. "What a funny question. Why not?"

"No, I want an answer. Why do you do so many things for him? You take him home with you lots of times. Drive him here from school. You study with him and come out here to work with him, when you don't have to. Why?"

Evan squatted down on his heels beside Annie, not looking at her but into the clear water. He swatted at the little minnows that raced out of his reach and circled curiously, just out of range. No use trying to hit them. They were too fast. I knew.

After a while, he answered Annie. His voice was slow and careful. "It's a hard question to answer, why you like somebody."

"Is it because he's a foreigner?"

Evan stared at her in surprise. "Why, Annie, I never thought about that. Maybe it is. I'm a foreigner, too, you know."

"You?"

"Sure. My dad came over here just after the war—the Second World War. He built up the grocery business. Then he went back to Greece to pick a wife. Grandfather wouldn't let Mother come to America until I was born. Said he'd never get to see his grandson any other way. I'm a naturalized citizen, just like T.C. will be, when he gets his papers."

"But you're different. You were raised here."

I could hardly hear his reply, Evan's voice was so quiet. "Not different, Annie. Just luckier." He was still for a long time, tossing pebbles into the water, always just missing the minnow he tossed at. In the quiet, I could hear the pines talking softly in high whispers, hear a blue jay calling, "Thief! Thief!" in the woods. I could hear the baying of dogs, the ripple of water, the plop of the pebbles. Finally Evan looked at Annie. "You asked me a hard question. Now let me ask you one. Why don't you like T.C.?"

Two pink spots came out on Annie's cheeks. She glanced at the jeep to see if I was listening, which, of course, I was. "I do like him all right. I mean, I try to be nice to him."

Evan snorted. "That's not good enough. Being nice to somebody doesn't count for anything. You are 'nice' to store clerks and servants, not to your kinfolks."

"He isn't my kinfolks!"

"That's what I mean. He's your adopted brother, a part of your family. But you won't accept that or treat him like a brother."

"Because he's not my brother. Petey's the only

brother I have. I never wanted any other."

"What about the baby?"

"Oh, well . . . he's a brother, too, but he's so little. He doesn't count, yet. Anyway, everybody loves babies."

"Not everybody." Evan shook his head. "I have an uncle who leaves home, every time my aunt has a baby. Doesn't come back until it's about a year old."

"I don't believe that!" Annie was aghast.

"True, though . . . and they have five kids. He likes them O.K. after they get bigger. Just can't stand babies. Suppose your dad had brought home a tiny baby, Annie. Would you like it any better?"

She drew a pattern in the sand with her finger, thinking. "I try, Evan. Sometimes I don't think it's T.C. that I don't like, really. He represents everything about war that I hate. Every time I look at him, I think about all the terrible things that have happened in that part of the world—Vietnam and Cambodia, and Dad getting wounded."

"You sound like Tanya. She's got snobs for parents, so you can't expect too much from her. Your parents are real people, Annie. Your dad is one of the finest men I've ever known. He served over there for years, and you don't blame him for it. If you do, you've really got your thinking fouled up. And it wasn't his own land. It *was* T.C.'s."

"Oh, now you sound like Petey. Anyway, I thought you and Tanya were steadies."

Evan pointed his finger at me and shot me with

his thumb. "Petey's a smart guy. You'd better listen to him, instead of that bunch you've been calling friends. No, Tanya thinks I'm going steady with Tanya. I'm not steady with anybody and not going to be until I finish college. Then"— he leaned back, resting his weight on one elbow—"I think I'll go back to Greece and get me a good, obedient little Greek maiden for a bride."

Annie couldn't tell if he was kidding, but she made a face at him. "Now you ARE kidding."

"Dead serious." He laughed. "And we're off the subject. It wasn't fair for you to blame T.C. for the whole set of problems in the Far East. He wasn't in the mess by choice. None of those people are."

"Neither was Daddy. But the scars on his legs are just as ugly."

"I don't think they're all that ugly," I said. Annie could be as nutty as she wanted to about T.C., but it wasn't right for her to take off on Dad. "Besides, it's time we went home. I have to help with the calves."

Evan helped Annie up. "Might as well. We're not communicating."

Which was an odd thing to say. They had talked and talked. As long as they talked about T.C., I had stayed quiet, hoping Evan could stuff some sense into her. After all, he had come to her rescue Saturday and again this morning. But I guess there was no use hoping. A normal girl would have flipped over Evan and would have been furious with me for breaking up their talk. Annie, who is definitely not normal, gave me what could only have been a grateful smile.

Evan shrugged in an "Anyway, I tried" gesture. I wondered if T.C. had asked him to talk with Annie. Odd. T.C. mostly worked out his own problems.

12

The Chief wasn't at the gate, as I had thought he would be. Instead, he was standing under the pine. Though he raised his head, shaking it up and down at Annie and whinnying as we drove up, he made no move to come to the gate.

"That was a short love affair." Annie grinned wryly at Evan as we climbed out of the jeep.

I wondered why he was standing so still. When Annie and Evan walked up to him, I trailed along. Evan began to laugh as they approached. Annie laughed, too. I couldn't see why at first, as I was behind them, but when they stopped I moved up. I laughed, too.

Brad had propped himself between the Chief's front

legs and was taking a nap. His head was resting against one hoof, and his arms were wrapped around the other. When Annie reached down and picked him up in her arms, he muttered and snuggled his face against her neck. He didn't wake up.

The Chief sniffed at the baby with his big nostrils flared in and out. He stamped his feet, probably to restore the circulation.

"I wonder how long he's been standing like that," Evan said.

Annie shook her head. "I wonder where Mother is. She never lets Brad out of her sight, unless someone else is with him."

They started back to the house. The Chief, seeing Annie's shoulder was occupied, stepped up to me and rested his head over my shoulder, instead. I rubbed his soft nose. "You *are* smart, Dogmeat. You'll take up with anybody, for a pat on the nose."

Annie looked back at me, shooting arrows with her eyes. "Don't call him that. He may not be a fancy riding horse, but he's a mighty good baby-sitter."

"And that's not bad," Evan said.

Annie rubbed her cheek against the back of the baby's red hair. "No, I guess not. He really is a special horse. That's what I wanted. A special horse."

"Absolutely Perfect Horse," I reminded her.

"No such critter," Evan said. "Not in man or beast. But each one has something special in it, one way or another. Just takes someone with special sight to see it."

"Each one special," Annie said thoughtfully. "You do see people like that, don't you?"

He shrugged and smiled. "Sure. You must, too; why else would you fall for a horse you knew you couldn't ever ride?"

"Because she's not always too bright," I muttered. Evan grinned back at me, though Annie didn't turn around.

At the gate, I tried to push the horse back while I closed it. He wasn't having any of that. He put first one big hoof, then the other, through the opening, while I pushed back. He wasn't rough, just definite. He wanted to come along, too.

"Annie!" I bellowed. "I can't make your horse stay in his pen!"

She looked back and chuckled, which didn't help my feelings much.

"Oh, let him come. He won't hurt anything."

"If he steps on any of Mom's flowers, she'll squash us both."

"He might eat 'em, but he won't step on 'em," Annie said.

I hoped she knew what she was talking about as I stepped out of his way and let the gate swing open. As soon as I started for the house, the old Chief forgave me and hung his head over my shoulder again. He wasn't a horse to carry a grudge.

Sure enough, he was careful of the flowers, putting his big feet neatly on the path right behind me. At the steps, I slid out from under his jawbone and

jumped up onto the porch. He looked at me reproachfully, but he didn't try to follow. He knew he couldn't
go into the house.

Evan laughed from the porch. "Makes you feel like
a dirty dog, doesn't he? Coming inside and leaving
him out like that."

"He's playing on your sympathy," Annie said, as
she disappeared into the house. We could hear her
calling, "Mom! Mom, where are you? Taro Chan?"

She came back onto the porch with a crease of worry
between her eyes. "I can't imagine where everybody
is."

"Don't worry," Evan said. "They're around somewhere. The station wagon's in the garage. Tractor's
in the shed."

"Pickup's gone," I observed.

"Thanks, chum," Evan said and frowned at me.
He was worried and trying not to let Annie know
it. I began to get scared.

The baby began to struggle to get down, and Annie
made him a lap to sit on. He rubbed his eyes and
stared at her sleepily. "Ann-eee!" he said, his voice
as sleepy as his eyes. Then, "Horseee!" and that was
excited.

"Horsey is right outside. And I do wish you could
tell me what you were doing out there and where
Mother is."

He made a hungry noise, and Annie said, "Petey,
get his cup and pour some milk in it."

I had done that many times. Brad took the cup
and crawled three legged to the screen door, patting

on it to be let out. When no one opened it, he sat down and began to chatter to the Chief through the screen in his own peculiar language.

"He's mighty good-natured when he wakes up," Evan said. "My little brother is such a grouch."

"He's in a good mood today. Not always. I think he knows he wasn't supposed to be outside with the horse, and he's not pushing his luck." Annie took a can of lemonade from the freezer and then put it back. She didn't seem to know what her hands were doing.

"Mom just has to be around somewhere," I said. "She wouldn't go off and leave Brad alone for long."

"Go look in the barn, Petey," Annie said. "I'm going to phone some of Mom's friends to see if she has called any of them."

Evan latched the screen door behind me, so the baby couldn't get out. "Look, Petey!" he said.

Through the trees, I got a glimpse of T.C. flying up the road. "It's T.C.," I said. "Where's he going?"

Evan pushed past me and ran onto the porch. "T.C.! Hey, T.C.!"

If he heard, he gave no sign of it. A red pickup turned into the road, and the driver slowed enough for T.C. to leap aboard. Then it took off at full speed across the field toward the Gopher Field.

I looked at Annie. She was as pale as I felt. "That's Dr. Kurt's truck," I said.

"Let's go see what this is all about," Evan said, scooping the baby up and putting him in Annie's lap as soon as she was in the jeep.

113

I led the Chief back to his pasture, and they picked me up at the gate. The Chief didn't object, this time. He hung his head over the gate and watched as we drove down the road and through the gap. He nickered once, behind us, complaining that he didn't like being left behind.

Evan followed the pickup across the pasture, splashing through the shallow creek, spattering us when he slowed to shift gears for the steep climb on the the other side. It had never seemed steep, coming at it slowly on the tractor. For the fast-moving jeep, the clay bank was an obstacle, as it must have been for the pickup we were following. Deep ruts had been gouged into the bank as it had gone up and over.

As we cleared the top, we could see the red truck behind a thin line of pines in the Gopher Field. The wire gap was open.

Two of the heifers huddled in a corner of the field, eyes wide, hides quivering. They were snorting. We didn't see any people until we stopped by the pickup. Dad, Mom, T.C., and Dr. Kurt were bent around a stuggling black calf on the ground. Dad was down beside the little bull, his knee on its neck, trying to hold it still, while Mom stretched one hind leg to full length and T.C. held the other. Dr. Kurt knelt beside the calf, working over him.

Evan leaped from the jeep and reached around Mom to take the leg from her. "Let me," he said. She turned loose and stepped back, as he took the strain.

"Mom . . . what's happened? What's the matter?"

Annie's voice was high and shaky, and I could feel my own legs quivering under me. There was so much blood on the ground and on Mom's dress, it was frightening.

"Honey, it's pretty bad." Mom wiped perspiration from her forehead with the back of her hand, leaving a dark smear. Her legs were splashed with the same bloody marks. "Sam heard the dogs again. They sounded close, so he came to see. He found the whole pack of hounds chasing the calves round and round the fence line, slashing at them all the time. One of the heifers was already down, and before he could scare them off, they pulled another one down and slashed the little bull. We're going to lose him, son. If Dr. Kurt can't stop the bleeding, we're going to lose him."

As we watched, the struggles of the calf became weaker and weaker. After a time, he was still. Dr. Kurt sat back on his heels and said, in a low tone, "I'm sorry, Sam. There just wasn't anything I could do. I tried."

Dad rubbed the short black curls on top of Mac's head. Then he stood, slowly. "I know, Kurt. I know." He looked at his bloody hands and turned away without looking at anybody. He walked over to the creek to wash his hands. He stayed gone a long time.

T.C. and Evan gently loosed the legs they were holding and stepped back. T.C. put a hand on my shoulder. "Easy, Petey. You look sick."

"So do you," I answered.

"I'm sure that is true. I feel sick," he said.

"Did you see the dogs?" Dr. Kurt asked Mom.

"No, but Sam got a good look at them. He said he thought they were going to tackle him, too, but they finally turned and ran into the woods when he yelled and threw rocks at them. He came to the house for the first-aid stuff and called you, and we left the baby asleep in the house and came to see what we could do. We met T.C. as he got off the bus."

Mom was really shaken. Ordinarily, she didn't talk much. Now she couldn't stop. Dr. Kurt knew it, too. He patted her on the arm.

"Why don't you and Annie go back to the house? This is no place to have the baby." He didn't wait for her to answer, just walked her over to our truck. She stood beside it, uncertain whether to leave.

Dr. Kurt didn't argue. He expected to be obeyed. He walked over to his pickup and spoke into his CB radio. When Dad come up from the creek, he said, "Sheriff's on his way out."

"Not much point in calling him, Kurt," Dad said. "I saw the dogs, but a hound looks pretty much like any other hound. Nothing I can prove except for the fact of two thousand dollars worth of dead meat." His voice was husky, and his eyes were strangely bright.

Dr. Kurt shrugged. "He needs to know what's happening. You want to butcher out these calves? We could save the meat."

"No." Dad shook his head. "I couldn't eat it." He looked at Mom, and she nodded agreement.

"T.C., you and Evan go get the big tractor. Put

the ditching blade on it. We'll bury them over by that bunch of pines."

"Right," Evan said. "I need to call my folks and let them know what's happening. We'll take the ladies back to the house now, if you like."

Mom started to protest, but Dr. Kurt interrupted her. "I've already suggested that. Susan, there's nothing more you can do here."

"Kurt's right, honey." Dad came over and put his arms around Mom, holding her very tight for a minute, then leading her back to the pickup. "Go on to the house with the boys. This is no place for Annie and Brad. Make us some sandwiches. We'll be hungry after a while.

"Petey"—Dad turned to me—"go with your mother. When the sheriff's car comes, bring him here."

I had opened my mouth to protest at the first sentence. I shut it at the second and climbed silently into the back of the pickup with T.C. Mom, with the baby in her lap, and Annie sat up front as Evan drove the truck back to the house.

It was a silent ride.

13

The Chief whinnied as we drove into the yard.

"Your baby-sitter's calling you," I said to Mom.
She looked questioningly toward Annie.

"You'll never guess where Brad was when we got
home," Annie said.

"I left him asleep in the house when Sam called
me," Mom said. "I knew you'd be along in a few
minutes."

Annie looked sheepish. We had taken entirely too
long in getting home, but she didn't mention that
now. It wasn't a good time to tell Mom. "He was
wrapped around the Chief's front legs. Sound
asleep . . . or pretending to be."

"I was in such a flurry, I guess I didn't lock the

door. Didn't you find my note? I left one telling you where we were and why. I didn't want you to come down there and see that terrible thing."

"We didn't see any note," I said.

"I put it on the table," Mom said, looking to see if it was there and we had overlooked it, like a couple of dummies. But it wasn't.

We looked under the table and all around the kitchen. When I heard the tractor start up, I left Mom and Annie still puzzling over it. I ran out and jumped onto the back of the tractor beside Evan.

T.C. swung by the gate, and I dropped off and hunkered down to wait for the sheriff to show up. From where I sat, I could see Annie coming out of the house with a bucket and what looked like a handful of cookies. It reminded me of my stomach. It didn't seem right to feel hungry after what had happened to our calves, but I felt totally hollow on the inside. I couldn't even remember what I had had for lunch. The thought of a cookie made my mouth water and conjured up thoughts of hamburgers and fries.

Annie carried the bucket into the Chief's shed, and I guessed that it was full of warm water for the bran mash she fixed for him in the evening. I wondered how bran mash tasted.

The sheriff's black-and-white Olds drove through the gate, pulling to a stop beside me. The deputy slid over and made room for me in the front seat. "You Mr. Braeden's boy?" he asked.

"Yes, sir. Petey." I had never talked with a sheriff before. It gave me the same feeling I had had when

Dad had introduced me to his admiral. Dry mouthed, I didn't feel like telling him that he was driving too fast. When he came to the creek, he knew. I had never heard tires squeal on dirt before.

"Any other way to get there, Petey?" he asked, looking at the steep bank.

"No, sir. They're right over the rise on the other side of the creek, if you'd rather leave the car here and walk."

He looked at me as if he had never heard of walking and put the Olds at the bank. It was built low to the ground. It scraped bottom, whined, and teetered uncertainly on the edge. He gunned it just at the right moment, and it plunged over with a roar, almost crashing into a stand of pine seedlings before he stood on the brakes and stopped the car so hard that its back wheels almost came off the ground.

"That's good for the machine," he said. He glanced at me, grinned, and winked. "County buys the cars, boy. Every year. It's a good lesson for you . . . don't ever buy an old county car at an auction, no matter how good it looks. We drive 'em."

"Yes, sir," I said. "You sure do."

The deputy laughed out loud, and the sheriff's grin broadened. "Now where are those calves?"

I pointed him through the stand of trees, until he got a glimpse of the pickup. That was all he needed. They went over to Dad and Dr. Kurt, and I drifted over to where T.C. and Evan worked with the tractor, cutting deeply into the red dirt to make a place for the wasted calves. There was nothing for me to do but watch. The two of them worked smoothly together, never getting in each other's way.

The four remaining heifers were huddled into a corner of the field near the gap. They didn't offer to move as I walked over to them. They snorted and trembled as I came up. After I had patted them and talked to them a bit, they gathered around me. They lipped at my fingers and licked my bare arms, so I knew that they were hungry. It was far past the time when they were always fed, but nothing could be done about that right now. Anyway, I knew Dad wouldn't leave them alone in this pasture. He would take them up to the barn lot for tonight, and they would go more readily if they were hungry.

Except for the grinding of the tractor and the low hum of voices by the truck, it was very quiet in the woods. The night creatures, disturbed at the beginning of their evening's activities by our presence, hadn't begun to make their twilight noises. The early locusts weren't zinging away nearby, though deeper in the woods their cousins were tuning up their eery song.

The peeper frogs along the creek let nothing disturb their singing, and after a while the bullfrogs added their bass rumbles to the soprano peepers' air. A mockingbird, whose territory included most of this pasture and the trees where the boys were digging, chacked and fussed as long as he could stand it. But mockingbirds don't hold grudges long, especially when they're nesting. He finally left the low branches and flew to the top of the tallest pine in his domain. There he began singing to his mate, flinging himself into the sky for a barrel roll now and again, when some brilliant passage of his own song completely overcame him.

I watched his performance until the sheriff's car drove away, followed by Dr. Kurt's red pickup.

Dad came over and sat down beside me, watching the mocker too, for as long as we could see him against the sky.

"What did the sheriff say, Dad?"

He shrugged. "I described the dogs and he said about what I thought he would. Still, he does know a couple of men who let their dogs run loose most of the time. He's going to talk with them and look over the dogs. Kurt's going along. He might be able to detect something."

"It's not fair. People just let those dogs out to kill whatever they find. It's not fair."

Dad put his arm around my shoulder. "I don't think they turn the dogs out to become killers, on purpose. I guess they think letting them run loose will keep them in good condition for hunting. Dogs in gangs are like people . . . they get into trouble when they're bored and undirected."

He sighed. "Anyway, Petey, who ever told you that life was fair? It isn't fair, and if you expect it to be, you're in for a lot of disappointment. We do the best we can with what comes our way, and that's all we can do. Don't ever holler, 'No fair.'"

He looked over at me. "You remember that little statue I have on my bedside table? The fat guy riding the mule backward?"

I nodded. "The Chinese type?"

"That's the one. He's a Chinese god—very ancient. I forget his name, right now, but it isn't important. His followers believe that events, the things that happen to people, aren't important by themselves. It's the way people react to them that gives them significance. Do you understand?"

"I think so. It isn't what happened to the calves that's the important thing. Just what we do about it."

"Right!"

"What *are* we going to do about it?"

He grunted, and I could feel the muscles in his arms tense. In the darkness, it was hard to tell what his expression might be. I surely couldn't read his voice. "What would you do, Petey?"

That was hardly a fair question. I couldn't do a thing, and he knew it. I shrugged, remembered that he couldn't see me any better than I could see him, and said, "I don't know. Shoot every loose hound I see, I guess."

"I'm angry enough to do just that," he said. Then he sighed again and said in a voice I couldn't recognize, "But like it or not, we've moved to this country to live, and we have to get along with the natives. We can't shoot every gook who wears black pajamas . . . some of those gooks are friendlies."

I didn't know why that frightened me so much. Dad almost never spoke of his service in Vietnam, and then only to tell some story that was sort of funny. I couldn't remember the time when he had been over there—I was too small. But this talk of shooting gooks and the chilled ice of his voice shook me up.

"What are *you* going to do, Dad?"

"Nothing, Petey. Nothing. I guess that's what hurts most of all. I'm not a do-nothing sort of man, son. When somebody hits my people, I want to hit back. But this time I'm going to leave it to the sheriff. Let the law handle it. I'm going to do nothing."

I never thought of Dad as someone who could be pushed around. The bitterness in his tone was disturbing. "Three dumb old calves. I guess they're not very important."

"Three dumb old calves? They're MY three dumb old calves. The foundation of our Angus herd. You loved those dumb old calves, didn't you? I did."

I didn't say anything. He knew. Somehow, it didn't seem like enough, just leaving it to the law. I wanted Dad to do something. Anything. Anything except sit here, the suppressed rage making him shiver in the darkness, making me afraid. And my fear made me even more afraid, because I wasn't sure just which frightened me most . . . my dad's reaction or what had happened to the little Angus calves.

14

T.C. called from the darkness, "This is finished. Is there anything else to be done?"

Dad pushed himself up. "No, nothing else. Let's catch up the heifers and take them to the barn lot."

That took a little time. We tied halters of rope around their heads, and Dad and I each led two. They weren't used to being led, but they didn't fight or pull back on the ropes. They seemed to be glad to be going with us. To stay in that pasture by themselves, after what had happened, seemed to be the last of their ambitions. T.C. led the way on the tractor, lighting our way, and Evan followed slowly, patting a balky calf now and again when one hesitated. Then Evan went back and got his jeep.

We put down fresh hay and feed pellets in the lot, but the heifers seemed too frightened to eat. Instead, they huddled in the shadow of the barn, making soft sounds deep in their throats. They trembled when one of us got close, unexpectedly. I hated to leave them alone, but if they weren't hungry, I *was.*

Or had been. Until I sat down. Mom had made sandwiches, a big plate of them, and a pitcher of lemonade. There were peanut butter and cheese, my favorite; peanut butter and strawberry jam, T.C.'s preference; plain cheese with butter, tuna fish, and something on that round brown bread that I wouldn't eat if I were starving. The others, except Dad, were at the table when I came in. I slid onto the bench and took a peanut butter and cheese off the tray. Funny how the filling was heavy and sticky. Hard to chew and harder to swallow.

Dad came out of his bedroom, his hair dark and glistening from the shower. He had on clean jeans and T-shirt, but he was limping and looked tired to the bone. He took one of those brown bread things. He didn't eat most of it, just broke it up and pushed the bits around his plate while the rest of us talked.

"What did the sheriff say, Sam?" Mom asked him at last.

Dad shrugged. "About all he could say. Nothing useful. He knows about the dogs running loose, but proving which bunch of dogs is something else again. Almost have to catch them on the place."

"Dr. Kurt went with the sheriff to check some of

the packs. Maybe he'll find some kind of proof," I offered.

Dad looked at me, but he didn't answer.

"You've been watching too many detective shows on TV," Annie said. "Did you expect him to take pawprints?"

"They might have blood on them, or something like that," I said.

"Sam, you ought to put out poison for them," Evan said, very softly. "A pack gone wild like that is dangerous to a lot of things besides livestock."

"I've thought about it," Dad said, his voice cold and hard sounding . . . something like branches that are loaded with ice, when they break in the wind. "When I was a boy in South Dakota, the wolvers came through, putting out bait. They got about three wolves for every hundred coyotes, foxes, weasels, and other little carnivores they slaughtered. And then the rabbits almost ate us off the land. There was nothing left to eat *them*. Bait would be a good thing if only you could make certain you'd only kill the animal you're after."

"What is the bait?" T.C. asked.

"Usually strychnine," Evan answered. "Remember your chemistry? C twenty-one, H twenty-two, N two, O two."

"Ah, yes. Poison from the nightshade family. I do not think much of poison, either. But perhaps a pit in the Gopher Field . . . they will likely come back looking for the rest of their prey."

"You've just been digging in that ground, T.C.," Dad said. "You want to dig a pit deep enough to catch a dog pack in that stuff?"

"No. The ground is very hard. It is not a good suggestion."

"It's a good suggestion, but the lay of the land is wrong. For a pit to work, you almost have to be in a heavy jungle where everything travels in set paths. This is an open field. There's just no way to make sure the dogs would go near it."

"Why don't you just lie in wait and shoot the dogs when they come back?" Annie asked.

"Annie!" Mom said, reproachfully.

"No, that's a good observation," Dad said. "I'd like to shoot them, Annie. But I'm not going to do a thing, for a while. Give the sheriff a chance. We'll play it cool for a bit." He looked over at me. "But I'd say that a smart man would keep his dogs up, after this."

The phone rang, and Annie answered it. She called Evan, who went into the hall to take the call. "Evan's mother is worried about him," Annie said, as she sat down again.

"I don't wonder," Mom said. "It's been hours since he called to tell them he'd be late. It's after ten. Past bedtime, you kids."

Evan came in, grinning sheepishly. "Gotta go. Mom's breathing fire."

"I'm sorry, Evan. We shouldn't have kept you so long," Dad said.

"Don't worry. It's her Greek blood. By the time

I get home, she'll be crying. Probably she'll call over here to apologize for calling me. Papa says that with a Greek woman, you have to be a turtle with a thick shell—and know when to pull in your head."

Dad stood up and held out his hand to Evan, as he did with grown-ups. "Evan, thanks. The boys and I could have done it alone, but it was good to have your help."

Evan took the proffered hand. "I'm glad to help, sir. I'll bring everyone home right after school tomorrow. There may be something else I can do."

We all followed him out to the jeep. From the direction of the Chief's pasture came the sound of his shuffling footsteps. There was a soft nicker. Annie walked over to the fence and stroked his nose.

In the reflected light from the porch, Evan's teeth gleamed white. "See you," he said, and started the engine.

15

Out of the darkness, the monkey-faced owl who lived in the rafters of the barn in daytime and hunted at night flew up with a startled whoop. He sailed through the lights toward the safety of the barn. As he lighted on the long pole above the hayloft door, he gave his scary call that sent shivers up my spine. To the owl, it was his own way of reassuring himself that everything was all right and nobody was chasing him. But it made my skin goose pimple.

To the little heifers below in the barn lot, it must have sounded like the dogs. They let out a panicky bawl and all four of them hit the fence as one, splintering the wooden rails and scattering in different directions in the darkness.

One of them thundered past me, eyes red and rolling in the jeep's headlights. I grabbed for her halter as she brushed past, missed it, and caught her tail as her hindquarters hit me in the chest. Her momentum pulled me against the jeep, and I lost my grip. She ran on down the road, and I sank down, speechless with pain, beside the jeep.

Dad leaped after one of the calves, and T.C. ran after another, while Evan jumped from the jeep, trying to catch the one I'd missed.

Mom ran to me. "Petey, are you all right? Here, let me see."

When she touched my shoulder, I hollered. I couldn't help it.

Very gently, she put her arm around my waist and helped me to the porch. She was leading me into the kitchen when Evan came back through the lights. He had his calf by the halter and the tail and was forcing her ahead of him toward the barn. He had a skinned elbow, and the knees of his jeans were torn.

T.C. soon came with another, holding it the same way, halter and tail. He wasn't as battered as Evan. The two of them went looking for the fourth calf, and for Dad, after locking their two in the barn. It was some time before the three of them came back with the two remaining calves. They stopped by the porch.

"How's Petey?" Dad asked.

"I think his shoulder may be broken," Mom said. "It's a bad bruise, and the joint moves oddly. It's very painful, too."

"Yeah," I said. "It does hurt."

The heifers were slavering white foam from their mouths and moaning with fear.

"Poor little critters," Evan said. "I never thought I'd see a cow with hysterics."

"Honey, what are you going to do with them?" Mom asked. "You can't leave them in that dark barn all night. They'll go mad with terror."

"Put them in with the Chief," Annie said. "He likes little things. I think he'd be good for them."

Dad nodded. "I think you're right."

They led the frightened calves over to the fence, where the Chief was pawing and snorting. Immediately, he put his head over the fence rail to smell them. They mooed and struggled. Then they began to pull toward him, trying to touch him with their noses. Annie opened the gate, and the men led the heifers inside.

The Chief seemed excited to see them, nickering softly, touching their backs with his nose, moving around them. T.C. and Evan brought the other two from the barn, and the old horse included them in his examination. He began to bunch them, moving around them in a circle.

"They'll be all right with your baby-sitter," Dad said to Annie. "Let's leave them now."

As soon as everyone was outside, and the gate closed, the Chief took over, keeping them in a secure knot. He began urging them up the hill, pushing on their rumps with his nose, crowding them with his chest toward the shed. He snaked his head and shifted his feet, the way a cutting horse is supposed to, pushing them in the direction he wanted them to go, without rushing them. They disappeared into the darkness of the shed. In a little while, the troubled murmuring of the heifers stopped, and everything was quiet.

"I'll be damned," Dad said, not apologizing for his language.

"Now that the crisis is over, I have to go, or I'll have to be rescued myself when I get home," Evan said. "I'll see you tomorrow. Hope that arm's not too bad, Petey."

"It'll be O.K.," I said. But I wasn't really convinced. By then, the thing hurt so bad that I was beginning to feel light-headed.

Evan waved good-bye and drove off, his headlights swallowed up into the night before the sound of his engine died away.

Dad must have heard something in my voice. He came over and squatted down beside me. "Where do you hurt?" he asked.

"All over," I answered truthfully. "But I think my shoulder's busted."

"If you're trying to get out of school tomorrow, forget it," he said and laughed. His hands were very gentle as they explored the injured shoulder. He put an arm around me when I began to sag.

My knees felt like wet newspaper, and my stomach was kind of squishy. I wasn't going to cry, no matter what, but the tears began to squeeze out, in spite of anything I could do to stop them. I really did *hurt*.

"I don't think it's broken," Dad said. "But we're

going to the hospital to have some X rays, anyway."

I wanted to say, "Wait until morning," for everyone looked so tired. The words just wouldn't come out. I knew Dad wouldn't wait, anyway. And there wasn't much point in waiting, not if it was going to hurt like this all night.

Mom called the doctor while Dad went for the pickup. "Are you worried about staying here with the baby?" she asked Annie when she hung up the phone.

"No. Of course not. T.C. is here," Annie said. "We'll be fine."

"I'll sleep on the couch until you get back," T.C. said. "I want to be downstairs."

"That's a good idea. Annie, you might like to sleep in our bed, to be near Brad. I don't know if you could hear him from upstairs, if he wakes up."

"Sure, Mom. Don't worry about anything. Take care of Petey. We'll be all right," Annie reassured her.

The two of them helped me into the pickup, and I sat between them, Mom cradling the injured arm gently next to her, protecting it.

It was a drive without conversation. The only thing I remember anyone saying was when we were about halfway there. Dad looked at Mom and said, "Quite a day! Quite a day!"

"I can do without another like it," Mom agreed.

At the hospital, they were waiting for us. Dr. Jerry Tucker was a young guy, tall and lanky. He seldom smiled. His mournful expression was generally enough to frighten his patients into doing anything he suggested. I knew that I never felt like arguing with him.

He made me feel as if I were at death's door. He examined me in the emergency room, lifting my arm and probing the muscle of my shoulder and back with his strong fingers.

"Sorry to get you out so late, Jerry," Dad said, after the preliminaries were over.

Dr. Tucker sighed. "Nothing ever happens to any of my patients in the daytime, during office hours." I sucked in my breath sharply, when he came to the touchy spot. He left off probing immediately and stuck a needle full of stuff into my arm, before I had time to dread it.

"Can't stand jumpy patients," he said. He went back to examining the shoulder, probing and moving it, after he'd given the drug time to work.

When they finally took the X rays, I hardly noticed, and by the time they decided what was wrong with me I was too sleepy to care. I hardly remember being carried back to the pickup with about fifty yards of tape wrapped around my shoulder. One arm was pinned to my body, I do recall. I surely don't remember being put to bed. Not until he climbed down from the top bunk the next morning did I know that T.C. had switched beds with me.

"What time is it?" I asked, when I could shake the fuzz out of my brain.

"Time for me to get ready for school and you to go back to sleep," he said.

135

"I'm hungry." I struggled to push myself into a sitting position without knocking my brains out on the bunk above. "I don't know why you like this bunk better than the top one. It's too squeezed in."

"I don't like or dislike either one. It's all the same to me, as long as I have a dry place to sleep. I hate sleeping on wet ground."

"Well, I'm glad you haven't any druthers," I said. "I don't like this one. Did you do that a lot?"

"What?"

"Sleep on the wet ground."

"Petey, even once is too much."

"But you did it more than once, didn't you?"

"Yes, Petey. More than once. Does your shoulder hurt much?"

"Only when I breathe," I muttered.

"You must be feeling better. You're grouchy," Mom said from the doorway. "Step it up, T.C. Breakfast is ready. You'll miss the bus."

"What about me?" I asked.

"You're going to get a few days off." She sat on the side of the bunk and examined the bandages, to see if they were still tight enough. "Dr. Tucker calls it a separation, and he said that that is sometimes a lot more painful than a nice clean fracture. Not to mention that it's a lot more trouble to heal well. So, Pete-my-Buck, you may just finish this term of school at home."

"Can you really *do* that?" A little pain, I figured, was a small price to pay for my freedom.

"We'll see," Mom said. "Annie's going to stay

136

home with the wounded and lame today, while I go into town to see your teacher to see what she has to say about it."

I leaned back on the head rail of the bunk. If Mom was going to ask Mrs. Reilly, I'd just as well put on my pants and go to school today. She wasn't going to look favorably on any plan that would keep any kid out of school, even if every bone in his body was separated. Oh, well. One day off is better than none.

"I'm hungry, too," I reminded Mom.

"Not much of a nurse, am I?" She smiled, pushed the hair out of my eyes, and cleared a place on my forehead for a kiss. "Feel like coming to the kitchen, or do you want breakfast in bed?"

I scrooched back a little more. "Can I have scrambled eggs?"

"Whatever you want—if we have it."

"Biscuits?"

Mom nodded.

"And bacon?"

Her eyes were twinkling, as she nodded again. Usually, we had oatmeal or something like that for breakfast on school days.

"Can I have some honey and some . . ."

"Hold it!"

Mom was laughing, now. "Don't push your luck, Petey. I'll send someone up here to start you off with some orange juice. After bacon and eggs and biscuits and honey, you'll just have to take potluck with the rest of us, if you're still hungry."

137

"O.K.," I said and grinned back at her. "A guy heals faster, though, when he has lots of good stuff to eat."

She left, laughing. I heard her say to Dad as she walked into the kitchen, "I don't know where he gets it. Certainly not from my side of the family. Your son is getting to be a first-rate con man."

Dad said something I couldn't quite hear. They laughed together, in that comfortable way that makes a kid feel warm and safe inside. Even if they are laughing at him.

16

Annie brought up the orange juice.

"How's old Dogmeat today?" I asked.

"Don't call him that. He's suffering from a bad case of divided loyalties. I took him his bran, and he just took little nips out of the bucket, instead of sinking his head into it up to the eyes, the way he did last night. He's got responsibilities."

"The little heifers are O.K.?"

"Fine. They mooed at me and kept the Chief between me and them. Even when I was brushing him down, they stayed on the opposite side and peeped at me from under his barrel. You'll have to come down and see after a while. It is so funny!"

"Is Dad going to leave them in there with him?"

Annie shrugged. "I guess so. Why not? They seem to like it . . . they're pretty well settled down, as long as nobody is in there with them. I know *he* likes it. I put oats in his bin, and the heifers started eating it. The Chief just lipped at their withers, the way he does with my fingers. It didn't bother him a bit when they started in on his breakfast."

Dad brought in the white bed-tray, loaded down with food. "Hey, Petey! How goes it today?"

"Sore. Hungry. That looks good."

"Your mother can spread a pretty nice breakfast, when she gets going." He laughed and left me to eat one-handed.

There were more biscuits than I could possibly have eaten by myself. Not out of a can, either. She had warmed the honey. There was a pile of golden scrambled eggs that must have been four or five, at the least. Besides the four slices of bacon, there was a glass of milk. On the side were butter, peanut butter, and half a dozen of those brown sugar cookies I like so much. My appetite didn't need any encouragement. I was hungry enough to manage one-handed very nicely—without help!

Once things quieted down, I slept until noon. Then I struggled into my pants by myself, but I couldn't figure out how to get into a shirt. Mom helped me into an old sports shirt of Dad's. She put it on the good arm and then buttoned it around the taped one. I looked into the mirror. If I'd had an eye patch, I'd have made a pretty good pirate.

"Dr. Kurt drove up a little while ago. He and Sam

are down at the barn," Mom said. "Annie's out with the Chief. If you'd like to go outside for a bit before lunch, you may."

Stiff as I was, I still thought going outside sounded good. Eveything is so green and fresh in May. New leaves everywhere, new grass. Flowers growing wild in the woods and the pastures and the yard. There was even a trumpet-shaped flower, all red-and-gold-colored, hanging out of the trees. I stood on the porch until I located Dad and Dr. Kurt by the sound of their voices, inside the barn.

I stopped just outside, not because I wanted to listen, but because it was one of those conversations you ought not to interrupt.

"I don't want this to come to a killing," Dad said.

"Neither does the sheriff, Sam. Nobody does," Dr. Kurt said. "I just thought I ought to tell you. Blackburn seems a good enough sort, but he's a mean man. He has already killed one man over those damned dogs. He served several years in the penitentiary for it, too. People walk shy of him, now he's out. Treat him with a lot of caution."

Dad's laugh was a short bark that I didn't like the sound of. "Kill one man! Kurt, what do you think I did in the Navy for those twenty years? Sat safely at sea pushing a pencil? I cruised up and down those muddy, fever-ridden rivers with the patrols. Every few days—sometimes every few hours—Cong or Khmer-Rouge or Communist Thai would come bursting out of the jungle at us. I couldn't possibly count the dead men I pin on my chest every time I put

141

on those five rows of ribbons. Even in the peacetime Navy there are hot spots, and as liaison with the patrols I was in the middle of them. 'Nam was the worst, but it wasn't the only.

"I wish I did have just one man to my account. Or none! That's why I want the sheriff to handle this thing. I don't want it to get too personal. I haven't been out of the Navy that long."

Dr. Kurt's jacket brushed against something as he shifted position. "Sam, I didn't mean that you couldn't do anything about it. I just thought you needed to know what kind of man we're dealing with."

"You sure it was his dogs?"

"Pretty near certain. There was a brindle bluetick, three Walkers, and a couple of redbones. Just the assortment you described. There were others, too."

"I didn't see all of them." Dad sighed. "I'm still going to let the law handle it, even if I have to go to court to make him keep the dogs up. I'm not going to let them chew up any more of my livestock, Kurt. I know ways to kill those dogs—tonight—so that nobody would ever know what happened to them. I don't want to do it that way. Not here. Not even with dogs. That's not what we came here for.

"Blackburn definitely said that he wouldn't pen them up?"

"Said he couldn't. Didn't have enough pens, and it ain't good for a hound to keep him tied all the time."

"Mine's not the only stock they've attacked. What's the fellow's name we stopped by to see the other night? Laney? I'll talk with him. See if we can get some kind of legal action going."

"And in the meantime, if they come back?"

Dad laughed again. That same ugly laugh. "They'll have to take their chances."

"You can't watch the stock all the time."

"I don't have to watch the Herefords. That old dirt kicker may look like a cube of fat, but he can handle anything that threatens his herd. Besides, they're fully grown. Those dogs haven't bothered anything but calves and young stuff. I'm turning the young Herefords out with the older stock for a week or so. I doubt that the dogs would come this close to the house to get at the little Angus heifers again."

"Doesn't seem likely," Dr. Kurt agreed. "What if they do, though?"

"The thirty aught six is in the kitchen, loaded. T.C. knows just where it is, and he's as good with it as I am. Maybe better. I expect Susan wouldn't be shy about using it, either, if she needed to. I think I'll call my lawyer this morning. See if I can go in this afternoon and talk to him about what steps we need to take."

Dr. Kurt laughed. "This is a very small community, Sam. I doubt that you'll have any trouble getting an appointment whenever you want it."

"Thanks, Kurt. I really appreciate everything you've done for us."

They were coming out of the barn now, and I didn't want to be found eavesdropping. I wandered across the back lot behind the barn. There was a little creek that, according to the man who sold us hay, had never been known to go dry. Once it had seeped all over the barnyard from a shallow channel, making a sort of marsh. Then it had spilled across where the front yard was now, near the house, and wandered away into the woods, through the pasture Annie had for her horse.

T.C. had taken that as his first project as soon as we had moved to the farm. All by himself, he had dug the channel deeper in the direction Dad wanted it to go. Then, together, the two of them had cemented those parts that seemed likely to wash and put gravel into the bottom of its muddy channel. Dad had had a pond dug in the big pasture, where we kept the Herefords. The creek filled that pond and kept it fresh, then ran away to wander freely through the woods beyond our farm.

At first, the pond had been red with mud. After a few months, it had cleared a bit, and now it was a good place to swim on warm afternoons in summer. The Herefords didn't seem to mind, either. Sometimes they joined the swimmers by wading deep into the water and making pointed remarks about creatures crazy enough to splash around in their drinking water. Only the bull sometimes objected.

Like today.

When I entered the pasture, intending to go down to the pond and sit for a while, he lifted his head and came over to see what I wanted. He wasn't ugly about it, but it was clear that I wasn't welcome. I left without any argument.

It didn't irritate me to be turned out of the pasture. It was the bull's business as a range bull to take care of his herd. "That old dirt-kicker," Dad had called him. Dad would stand beside him, rubbing the itchy places behind his horns and talking, while the bull rumbled softly in his throat, as if he were answering. It always looked as if they were discussing the herd.

Mom didn't like for Dad to make so free with the bull. She was afraid of him and said so frequently, though he had never in any way offered to hurt anybody. But she was right about one thing. It was wise to take care around him. He was just so darn *big* . . . he could step on you absentmindedly and squash you flat, before he even knew you were there. T.C. regarded him with admiration from a great distance. Annie never went into the pasture to swim unless Dad was along.

Mom called us for lunch. "Where *were* you?"

"Oh, just around," I said. No need to get her started. My going into that pasture without Dad was one of her pet peeves.

After lunch, Dad went to town, and Annie sat feeding the baby. I helped stack the dishes with one hand and tried to look pitiful. Mom ignored that. She always knew when sympathy was merited.

When we had finished, she asked, "Annie, would you mind staying close to the house this afternoon? I'm going to town, and I don't want Brad wandering around unsupervised. Your horse wouldn't hurt him, but the calves might step on him."

Annie laughed at the thought. "Sure, Mom. I have

to study, anyway. Can I take him out to the pasture with me when he wakes up?"

"If you're careful. The Chief has the heifers to look after, now. He might not have time to be such a good baby-sitter today."

"I'll be careful."

"I'll see that she is," I added.

"You. Go and lie down for a while." Mom pointed her finger at me. "You can get up when the baby finishes his nap."

Objections did no good. When I got all stretched out, I was glad Mom hadn't listened. My shoulder ached deep down, as well as twinging sharply when I moved quickly. It was good to lie back and relax.

There are noises on a farm to listen to when you are quiet on a lazy afternoon. If you don't want to lose yourself in a book, and there's no good music on the radio, and there's nobody to talk to, you can just listen.

Annie was in the porch swing. The chains creaked as she gently pushed herself back and forth. I knew she was deep in her studying, not even aware that she was moving. Cow sounds came faintly from the pastures, mingled with the voices of birds and the distant whine of trucks passing on the highway. There was just enough wind to set the trees to talking. The oaks and gums gossiped and chattered. The dignified pines shushed everything and sighed, occasionally, with what seemed outraged dignity.

I like the pines best. They stand so tall and straight and they mind their own business. That old pine out in the Chief's pasture is so large I can't reach around it. Yet it's a friendly-feeling tree, pleasant to lean against, with soft needles fallen around its base, for sitting on. It smells clean and resiny on a hot afternoon.

Some of the kids claim they chew the yellow, sticky gum that seeps out of sweetgum trees when you make a deep cut in the bark. I tried that once. It stuck to my teeth and didn't taste all that good, either. I'll take bubble gum or Doublemint, any day.

Beneath all the sounds I listened to, I was vaguely aware of another sound. It was too faint to identify, but it nagged at me like a name I couldn't remember, or the date John Adams became President. (I missed that on a test just last week.) The sound drifted around under all the other sounds, and finally it faded away. I forgot about it as I listened to the vocal battle between a meadowlark that had come too near the house and the mockingbird whose territory he had invaded. I finally drowsed off to sleep, listening to those nutty birds screaming at each other.

17

"Hey!" Annie was bent over me, poking my chest while one braid tickled the end of my nose. "Wake up! Brad and I are going out to the Chief's pasture for a while. Want to come along?"

"Sure. Anything to get out of the house. You through studying?"

"No, but the baby's awake. And the sun is gorgeous. A shame to waste a day like this studying. I can do the rest tonight."

"You going to school tomorrow?" I tested the stiffness of my shoulder and didn't think I'd be going anywhere tomorrow.

"I guess so. Unless Mom needs me at home."

"Your grades aren't all that great. Isn't it going

to mess you up, missing so much?"

Annie gave a funny little shrug. "I'm passing every-thing. I doubt that these few days will cause me much trouble. Next week, now, when we're reviewing for finals . . ." She didn't finish. No need to. That is one thing good about being in the lower grades. No finals.

Annie went out with Brad and left me to get up at my own speed. Which was a good thing, because my speed wasn't anything to brag on. I seemed to be getting stiffer and sorer, instead of better. When I finally got to the kitchen, I found the plate of cookies and the glass of orange juice Annie had left on the table for me. When I finished the juice and rinsed out the glass, I stuffed cookies into the pocket of Dad's shirt and followed her out to the pasture.

The baby was hanging on to one of Dogmeat's legs. The horse was lipping at the top of his head. When I came close enough, he reached out and blew on me through his big nostrils. I rubbed him between the eyes briefly, before sliding down beside Annie. I set my back to the big pine.

"It's nice out here," I said.

"Um-hum," Annie agreed, her eyes on her book. I shut up and watched Brad. It didn't seem like such a good idea, letting him wander around under the horse like that. But if Annie wasn't worried, I wasn't going to be. He wove in and around the horse's feet and front legs, babbling to him as if he expected to be understood. The four black heifers weren't willing to go far from their watch-horse. Still, they didn't

149

want the baby close to them. They stayed just out of his reach, kinking their tails and making short runs away, when he reached for them. The baby crowed and laughed at their antics. He tried to coax them to play with him, but they weren't having any. It was a game to him. When he tired of it, he left the horse and crawled down the hillside toward the shallow creek.

"Brad's wading," I said, when Annie didn't seem to notice.

She grinned at me over the book. "I know. I'm watching. Won't hurt anything. Don't get your bandage wet."

It's hard to wade without getting wet. I walked down to where Brad squatted. He was getting his tail wet while he patted at the surface of the water, soaking himself. I made him some leaf boats and tried to communicate. He might have been a Martian, for all the sense he made. Still, for all his language problem, he was a pretty smart kid. He didn't smash the leaf boats. He followed them along, freeing them when they caught on the bank of the creek.

When one would finally race out of his reach or the breeze would capsize it, he would come back to me. He'd say something that I generously took to be "'Nother boap!" I would give him another "boap," and he would follow it until it, too, was gone.

We played by the creek for a long time before Annie came down. "You two come back up the hill and sit in the sun. I'll go make us some peanut-butter sandwiches."

"Put cheese on mine," I said.

"I know, I know. Come on, Brad. Out of the water."

"NO!" That was clear enough. He turned back to his last boat.

"Peanut-butter-and-jelly sandwich?" Annie said, with a promise in her voice.

"No," he said again, but not as definitely, this time.

"Peanut-butter-and-jelly and milk?"

"No."

"Peanut-butter-and-jelly and Coke?"

"O.K.," he said cheerfully. He waded out and followed me up the hill to the spot where the pine shade began. We sat in the sun, making a house out of the thick pine needles. We'd push them around to form rooms. The cones made fine furniture. It was mostly my project, with Brad handling the cones very gingerly. He didn't like the stickery points.

Old Dogmeat and the heifers came over to watch. They nosed at the needle walls and made doors where no doors were supposed to be. The horse finally came around to stand behind me. He breathed on my neck, with his nose resting on my good shoulder. It didn't mean anything, but it was kind of nice, just the same.

Annie came onto the porch with a big tray. Just as she started down the steps, the phone rang. She put the tray down on the swing and went into the house. When she came out, she was smiling.

At the gate she called to me, "Mom has a flat. She's going to be late getting home, and she wants me to start supper. Why don't you bring Brad in and put some clean clothes on him, while I get started?"

"One handed? I can't dress him when I have both hands free and a knee in his chest. Where's my sandwich?"

"Well, peel him down and dry him off. I'll do the rest. Come in to eat your snack. I ought to make something for the boys. Mom said she saw Evan and T.C. pass the station. They'll be home in just a little while."

I coaxed and dragged Brad back to the house, grumbling under my breath about my sandwich getting soggy, my shoulder aching, and the fact that I couldn't latch the gate properly with one hand. Not while blocking Brad out of it with my body and tugging on the gate at the same time. I finally gave up on the gate, satisfied when it stayed shut, and hauled the squealing baby into the house.

"Petey, you don't have to be so rough with him!"

"*You* don't have to be rough with him," I said, panting with effort and exasperation. "He won't come with me, and I can't pick him up and carry him."

"I'm sorry, Petey." Annie came to my rescue. "I forgot about your shoulder. Sit down and eat your sandwich. I'll clean him up before I get started in the kitchen."

She took the struggling baby into his room. I could hear her singing and talking to him to soothe him. I had really bruised his feelings. He was not a kid who liked being dragged around. I know better, too . . . I don't know what makes me do things like that, now and again.

152

I finished my milk and sandwich and was in the bathroom when I heard Annie sit down at the table with the baby. By now, he was laughing at some silly thing she was doing to amuse him.

Then the phone rang, and I knew from the conversation that it was Dad, wanting to talk to Mom.

"She's at Red's Service Station," Annie said. "She has a flat tire. They're going to patch it for her while she waits. The spare was flat, too."

Annie laughed at something Dad said. "But we're perfectly all right. We've been out in the pasture with the Chief. Now we're having snacks before I start supper for Mom. Anyway, Evan and T.C. will be along in a few minutes. Mom saw them pass the station in the jeep. Don't worry about us."

I tried to remember when Annie started calling him T.C., like the rest of us did, instead of Taro Chan. It must have been recently, because I hadn't noticed, before.

While Annie was still talking, I heard the door close softly. It wasn't T.C. and Evan coming in, because they would have made a lot more racket. I hadn't heard the jeep drive in. I hadn't latched the screen door, so I knew it must be Brad sneaking outside again. He would get right back into a mess.

It took me a minute to get my shirt buttoned and arranged. Then I started after him. I was in the kitchen when I heard the first yelp of the dogs.

18

For an instant, I couldn't move. Of course! Dogs! That was what I had heard while I was resting, earlier in the afternoon. Far off. Faint. Dogs hunting.

They had probably been in the Gopher Field, then casting around looking for the rest of the calves. Something had probably drawn them off, pulled them farther away from the house and out of earshot. A luckless rabbit, maybe. Or a deer.

Now they were back . . . out there in the yard. With the baby!

Then I could move. "Annie! The baby's outside!" I yelled, knowing that she must have heard the dogs. I didn't wait to see what she'd do. I didn't even think of how little I could do, in the shape I was in. I just hit the screen door with my good arm and came off the porch in two steps. I grabbed the broom as I ran past it.

Brad was screaming with fear. The pack—there must have been eight or nine dogs in it, though I didn't take time to count—had him backed up against the gate. They were looping and weaving around him, snapping at him now and again. There was a bloody gash on one side of his head as if one of the dogs had grabbed at an ear and missed its hold. There were other gashes on his fat legs and on the arms that he had instinctively held up before his face. Only the fact that he had set his heels stubbornly into the sand, pushing his back against the slats of the gate, had kept them from dragging him down.

The heifers weren't in sight, as I hurtled toward Brad. But the old Chief was on the other side of the gate. He was snorting and prancing, his ears back. The dogs paid no attention to him. He was too big for their use. They wanted something little. Something they could maul to death. Like Brad.

I landed in the middle of the pack, swinging the broom like a flail. A couple of good whacks sent the dogs backing off, startled. But they weren't through. They seemed to sense that there wasn't anything much that I could do to them. Perhaps they could see that I was wounded. Whatever it was, they decided that they could take me on, too. I could see it in their eyes. They started toward me, heads down, lips curled back over their teeth, the fur along their skinny backs standing up stiff. It was a thing I'll never forget as long as I live.

I've never been so scared. For the first time, I realized how futile the swinging broom handle was against a pack of determined and hungry dogs. I backed against the gate, squeezing the baby behind me against it, so the dogs couldn't get at him. I wedged him in tightly and kept swinging the broom. Suddenly, the gate that I hadn't been able to latch properly earlier gave way. Brad and I were dumped into the dust at the Chief's feet.

The dogs leaped forward as I fell, and I felt their teeth close on me. Especially my legs. I yelled and folded up around the baby as well as I could. I screamed again as one of the dogs sank his teeth into my bandaged shoulder.

That dog was suddenly lifted from the pack and flung, screaming, through the air. He landed in a sodden heap beside the fence. The old Chief was standing over us like a maddened shadow. He was striking out with his hooves, biting, kicking. He didn't look old, from where I lay curled in the dirt. He looked like a wild horse, his eyes red, his lips pulled back from his gums. Sounds came out of him that I'd never heard a horse make, not even in the movies. Sounds I never wanted to hear again.

He fought as I'd imagined wild stallions fought off wolf packs on the plains, in centuries past. Yet, although he seemed to be standing directly over us, he never so much as nicked us with one of his hooves.

The only thing that touched me was his tail, which snapped across my face when he whirled to meet some new threat from the dogs.

Three of the dogs were down, unmoving. The others started to back away, raging, fearful now of the horse. The Chief snaked his head along the ground, his legs set wide, balancing so as to meet his attackers from any direction. He challenged them again with one of those deep, whistling screams, and the dogs broke. They began to back away, snarling.

With everything that had happened right on top of me, I hadn't heard the jeep drive up. But now T.C. and Evan were there. T.C. had Dad's rifle. I saw a black-and-tan hound leap into the air and collapse before I heard the first shot. With the second, a red hound plunged forward, his front legs seeming to melt under him, his bloodied muzzle digging a furrow into the loose, pawed dirt. The Chief squealed again, snaking his head toward the three remaining dogs. They took off running for the woods. T.C. shot twice more, and only one dog disappeared into the trees.

The Chief stood snapping his mane from side to side for a moment longer. Then he visibly relaxed and came over to sniff at me, seeing if I was all right before walking out of the gate to see about Annie. He actually seemed to be checking us all out.

I hadn't even thought about Annie. She was in the fight, too. Now she was sitting in the dirt with tears running down her face. Her forearm was a bloody mess, where one of the dogs must have grabbed her when she waded in to help me. She wasn't quite as chewed as the baby and I were, because by the time she had told Dad what was happening, the Chief was taking care of a lot of the action.

"He fought them off," she said to nobody in particular in a funny, tight voice. "He fought them off."

"Annie, are you all right?" T.C.'s naturally pale face was altogether without color. He didn't seem to have any features except his very black eyes and the two smudgy lines of his eyebrows. The rest was just a blur.

"That was some shooting," Evan said. He put his hand on T.C.'s back. I think he was tactfully steadying him.

"Four in four shots," Annie said in the same funny voice. Her eyes were wide as she looked at T.C.

"I'm sorry, Annie. It's something I learned a long time ago."

"I'm not sorry," she whispered fiercely. "I'm not sorry at all!" She took his hand and came over to where I sat in the dirt holding the screaming baby. "They would have killed us, if it hadn't been for you and the Chief. He fought them off, and you shot them."

Evan looked at the dogs that the Chief had tossed away. "Look," he said as he touched the dog. Its head lolled limply. "He broke their backs as he tossed them off."

Annie shuddered. "I want to go into the house. T.C., would you bring the baby?" She didn't wait to see if he did, or even to look at me to see how badly I was chewed up. She just walked into the house, holding her bleeding right arm with her left hand.

Evan and T.C. looked at each other and then at me. "Shock," T.C. said. "She'll be all right, Petey. It's something that happens after a battle, sometimes. Can you walk?"

"Sure," I grunted. I tried to stand, after he lifted Brad out of my arms. My shoulder kind of exploded, and my stomach turned over a couple of times. I sat back down. "In a minute, maybe."

"Maybe, nothing," Evan said. He slid an arm around my back, being careful of my shoulder, and the other arm under my knees. He lifted me as easily as T.C. had picked up the baby. It would have been humiliating if I hadn't felt so weak.

I looked back over his shoulder at the Chief, as he carried me away. Now he didn't look like a wild horse. He looked old. Older than he ever had. He turned and walked toward his shed, where the little heifers waited. He stumbled as he walked.

"Should I take Petey up to his room?" Evan asked T.C.

"No," I said. "I don't want to get blood all over the sheets."

"Forget the sheets," T.C. snapped.

"No, really!" I insisted. "Put me down by the table. You can clean up the mess better there."

"I think we'd better take the three of you to the doctor, right away," Evan said.

Annie met us at the door. "T.C., you hold the baby while I see how badly he's hurt. Evan, you can clean up Petey, can't you?" She had already washed her arm and wrapped some gauze tightly around it as a compress.

There were bandages on the table, where she had them ready, as well as antiseptic. She took over, washing the baby with light dabs of clean cotton, talking to him, trying to quiet his cries enough to tell if he was really hurt or just frightened. Once or twice, she glanced my way or looked at T.C. Her expression was odd—sort of round-eyed.

I couldn't pay much attention to her. I had troubles of my own. Evan was as gentle as he could be, dabbing at the dirt and blood with antiseptic-dampened gauze. But it burned something fierce, and some of the gashes in my legs were deep. The pants were a total loss, unless we cut them off at the hips and used them for a bathing suit.

"Little buddy, you're going to need some major repairs on those legs," Evan said. "How about your shoulder? The bandage is all bloody. Did one of them get you there?"

"Yeah," I said, remembering how the Chief had grabbed that dog and flung him through the air. "He didn't have time to bite through to hurt," I said, between clenched teeth, "but I think the Chief pulled him off before he worried his way through the bandage."

There was the sound of cars outside, and Dad's feet hit the porch, almost before the engine died. Mom was half a step behind him. She gave a funny cry when she saw what a mess we all were in. She grabbed

160

up the baby, who started wailing at the top of his voice all over again.

Annie told them the story. The boys filled in the details, because about then I was feeling light-headed again. I didn't remember until later that it was Evan who carried me outside and climbed into the back of the pickup, still holding me in his arms. T.C. got in back with us, and Annie and Mom, still clutching Brad, went into the cab with Dad.

We met the sheriff at our front gate. He didn't even wave us down, just took one look and whirled his car around in the road. He passed us with his siren blaring and his red lights flashing. Dad moved up to his back bumper and stayed right with him all the way to the hospital. It was the kind of ride I'd like to take sometime when I feel like enjoying it.

The sheriff must have radioed ahead, because there were doctors and nurses waiting on the emergency ramp when we pulled up to the hospital. Somebody shoved a needle full of sedative into me before I had time to object. What happened after that, I can't say.

19

I felt cold. I had been sitting out on a wild, nighttime
prairie, and there was a campfire, but it wasn't giving
out any heat. Only a blue, flickering light. The reason
I was cold was that all my clothes were gone. A piece
of stiff animal skin with hair on it was wrapped around
my middle and hung almost to my knees. It would
have been funny, except that there were other people
around the fire, and all the men had on the same
kind of rig. I looked again. The ladies did, too.

Nobody was saying anything, just passing around
some roasted bones and grunting at each other. I
wanted a bone, too, but they wouldn't offer me one.
I was scared to ask.

One of the men threw his bone into the fire and made a "listen" sign. Suddenly, the whole bunch of us were surrounded by silent wolves. Great gray wolves, with little slanty red eyes and long, yellow teeth that showed when they rolled their snarling lips back. Everybody pulled in closer and closer to the fire. One by one, they disappeared into the flames, leaving me alone in the wolf circle.

I picked up the bone somebody had dropped and held it like a club, knowing that it was no weapon at all, just a gesture. It turned soft in my hands, dripping off my fingers like an ice-cream cone in summertime.

From out of the darkness, the old Chief thundered up. Not old anymore. Not ugly and bony. As he must have been, young and wild, on the plains. He flung himself among the wolves, biting, kicking, screaming. The suddenness of his appearance was too much for me. I fell back into the fire.

The cold fire wasn't cold anymore. Now it was intensely hot, searing my shoulder. I tried to get away from the flames, but I couldn't move. I kept calling to the Chief to come and get me, but he was too busy fighting the wolves to hear.

Then the wolves were gone, as silently as they had come. Gone. The Chief was holding on to my arm with his lips—the good arm, not the burning one—shaking it gently. He let go and reached up to lip my cheek with his soft, velvet muzzle. Then he faded into the darkness. The Chief was gone. I was alone.

"Pete. Pete! It's all right now, Petey. It's all right. Wake up. You're having a bad dream." Dad's voice came through at last.

I opened my eyes, blinking to bring things into focus. I clutched his hand tightly. "Dad?" My voice sounded funny, even to me.

"Right here, Pete."

"Where are we?"

"In the hospital. You guys were chewed up pretty bad. They've practically given over a whole floor to Braedens."

"Where's T.C.? And Evan? Were they chewed up, too?"

"No. They're fine. They're home, taking care of things. Mom wouldn't leave you kids for anything, and neither would I. Mom's down in the next room with Annie and Brad."

"I want to see them. The baby looked awful. His ear was cut."

"Not just cut, Pete. Pretty nearly torn off. But that Jerry Tucker is a good doctor. All the time he was stitching you up, he was showing me how he was putting the skin together so the scars won't be too bad, when you've healed. Annie and Brad are all right, Pete. Really."

"I want to see," I insisted.

"It's about three in the morning. If I push you down the hall now, some white-skirted bureaucrat is going to descend on us. Can you wait until morning?"

"I guess so. If you're sure they're all right."

"They are. Thanks to you. You got the worst of it, brudder."

"I couldn't do anything," I said, remembering with shame how futile the broomstick had been against the raging dogs. "If the Chief hadn't been there . . ." I didn't finish. The dogs and wolves of my dream suddenly melted together, and I shuddered. "I was dreaming about it."

"I know," Dad said. "The old Chief must have been something else, out there."

"He was great, Dad. I'll never tease Annie by calling him Dogmeat again. He looked like a wild stallion. He stood right over us and never touched us with a hoof while he was whirling around and fighting off the dogs."

"Annie told us. She also said you went off the porch and waded into the dog pack as if you'd been the U.S. fleet. The Chief couldn't get at them until you opened the gate. Annie grabbed the gun and brought it out, but the dogs were all over you, and she couldn't get a clear shot. She was using it like a club when T.C. grabbed it away from her. By then the Chief had driven them back, and he could get a good shot."

The door opened quietly, letting in the brighter light from the hall. A nurse put her head in and said, "Mr. Braeden, the sheriff is here."

"It's all right," Dad said. "Petey is awake. Ask him to come in."

She pulled her head back, and the sheriff came into the room. He walked softly, for such a big man.

165

"How goes it?" he asked me, with a nod in Dad's direction.

"I'll be all right. All right, that is, for somebody that was almost dogmeat."

"Too bad that had to happen," he said, looking at Dad. "But sometimes it takes a near tragedy to get results. I've been on the phone to our state representative. The next time we get up a petition in this county to outlaw deer packs and to make people keep their hounds penned, he won't dare to shelve it, as he did the last one. That's been our main problem. The only way to stop it is by state law. The representative runs his own pack of hounds, and he just doesn't listen real good to the people who want it stopped. I'm going to count on you to help get signatures on our petitions."

"You know you have it," Dad said. "Plus anything else you need. That one pack won't bother anybody else, but there are a dozen other ones out in the woods, worrying the wildlife. Probably the livestock, too."

The sheriff shook his head. "I doubt that there are a dozen packs that run loose like that. Most folks keep 'em up. But the day of the deer hound is about over. It's a shame, in a way. At one time, people needed dogs to trail for them in these deep woods, to bring out the game. It's a tradition . . . used to be a necessity, when folks had to have venison for meat. Now most of the deep woods are gone, and using dogs is dirty pool."

"We see a deer, now and again, on our place. Not

as many as Susan remembers when she was young,'' Dad said.

"Not all that many left,'' the sheriff said. "Over-hunted. Too many people with guns. Not enough woods. These big rifle clubs keep yelling about keeping down the overpopulation of deer. I don't know how it is in other counties, but overpopulation is no problem here. If it keeps on the way it's going, pretty soon, there won't be any deer at all. Be extinct, like the dodo.''

"Did you get anyone to claim those dogs?'' Dad asked.

"Oh, they were Blackburn's, all right. He'll be over to see you in the morning. He'll pay damages for the calves. Pay these hospital bills, too, I expect.'' His smile had no humor in it, and I decided I wouldn't want him mad at me.

"Would he have paid for the funeral, if the dogs had killed one of my people?'' Dad asked, his voice grim.

The sheriff didn't answer, just shook his head. "He said he had a young Morgan horse—colt, rather—that he was going to give your girl, to replace the old horse.''

A big, cold icicle laid itself right along my backbone and set me to shaking. I looked at Dad and saw the tightness in his face. My voice came out in a whisper. "What happened to the Chief? He's dead, isn't he?''

Dad nodded, slowly. "Kurt took the boys out to the farm, after we saw you were going to be all right.

They went out to see the Chief. He was down on the straw in his shed. The little heifers were snuggled up all around him as if they were trying to keep him warm."

I didn't say anything. The tears rolled out of my eyes. I didn't try to stop them. I just kept feeling the soft velvet of his muzzle on my cheek when he came to say good-bye.

"Pete." Dad touched me lightly on the good shoulder. "Pete, don't feel bad about him. He put out everything he had, fighting off the dogs, because you were his people. His old heart had been beating for a long time. It just couldn't take a strain like that. There wasn't enough left to keep it going."

"Does Annie know yet?" I managed to ask.

"I wanted to tell you both in the morning," Dad answered.

"Maybe I'd better tell her," I said. "Early, before someone lets it slip."

The sheriff shifted uncomfortably. "Sorry about that, Pete. I thought you knew."

"I think you're right, Pete. You're the best one to tell Annie. If you don't mind," Dad said.

"No, I don't mind," I said. I closed my eyes.

Dad and the sheriff went outside and talked in voices I couldn't quite hear. When Dad came back into the room, I pretended to be dozing. He sat in the big chair beside the bed and dropped off to sleep, snoring softly.

I lay there, thinking about the dogs and the Chief. I felt as if I had swallowed a Popsicle whole, and it was lodged with the cold part in my stomach and the two little sticks stabbing me in the heart. The pain was worse than the dog bites on my legs. The doctor had given me a shot for those.

There wasn't any easy cure for this pain. I lay there with my throat burning, tears stinging my eyelids and rolling hotly down my temples.

Was it stupid to cry over a dumb old dogmeat horse that wasn't even mine? In the end, he'd been mine as much as anybody's. Anyway, he thought I was his, which is about the same thing, isn't it?

I lay there and tried to think how I was going to tell Annie. And wished that daylight would come. After a while, I slept.

20

Dad had gone, when I woke. A nurse came in and started stirring things up. When she brought my breakfast tray, Dad came with it.

"Annie's in much better shape than you are, Pete. The doctor is going to let her go home this morning. But she'll be in to see you, as soon as she finishes her breakfast."

"Could she come eat with me?" I asked.

"Can't think of any good reason why not. I'll ask," he said. He disappeared again.

In a couple of minutes, the door opened. Annie came in, pushing her bed tray before her. "Dad said you wanted company. How do you feel?"

"I hurt," I said, with complete honesty.

"The rest of us are going home this morning. Are you coming too? You look awful."

"Thanks a lot," I said. "How would I know? They don't tell me things like that."

"You must not hurt much. You're grouchy."

"I'm not grouchy. I have a lot on my mind."

"What mind?" Annie chuckled.

"All right," I said. "All right. Are you going to eat or fight?"

She laughed and took the silver lid off her eggs. "Petey, you really are a dumb kid. What made you wade into those dogs like that?"

I pushed my eggs around on the plate. "I didn't stop to think how dumb it was. I couldn't stand there and do nothing. Anyway, it never occurred to me that dogs would really attack a person. I never expected it. The dogs I know don't bite people."

I took a bite of the eggs and put the fork down. "Besides, it's like they say in the cowboy shows—'a man has to do what a man has to do.' "

Annie laughed at me. Not making fun, a serious kind of laugh. "I wasn't all that smart, myself. Even if I'd known how to use that gun, there was no way to get a shot. There was just a big tumble of boys and dogs . . . until that gate came open. How did you get it open, anyway?"

"It wasn't latched. I couldn't fasten it right when I dragged Brad up to the house. It was just kind of caught by friction. I thought we were goners, when it opened up behind, and we fell down."

"Goners!" Annie snorted. "I never saw anything

like the Chief. He just seemed to go wild. When you hollered, he picked up one of those dogs, shook it, and threw it thirty feet away. I never saw anything so magnificent. I even dreamed about it last night."

She sounded so proud and excited that I felt all sinky inside. "So did I. Only it was wolves instead of dogs. It was like a long time ago, and he was a wild horse. When he drove the wolves off, he lipped me on the face and kind of faded away." My voice faded and cracked.

Annie studied me. "What's the matter, Petey? Something's wrong with the Chief?"

I nodded. "His heart was too old, Annie. He fought with everything he had. There wasn't anything left when he had driven the dogs off."

"Oh, Pete!" Annie said. She didn't cry or anything. Not then. With her hand shaking, she put the lid back on the cold eggs and shoved the bed table away. For a little while, she stood looking out of the window at the little park on the hospital grounds, where the squirrels played in the early morning sunshine. Finally, she turned back to me. "Petey, when did Dad tell you?"

"Last night. He was going to tell both of us this morning, but the sheriff came by and let it slip. I wanted to tell you. I didn't do it very well, did I?"

She moved away from the window and hitched herself up onto the bed beside me. She sat, legs dangling. "You did O.K., Petey. There isn't any good way." Then she just sat, not looking at anything. Sitting still.

After a bit, I said, "You O.K.?"

"Yeah. I'm O.K. I was just thinking about things—how everybody laughed when I bought him. Now, when nobody would make fun of him anymore, he's dead."

"Do you really care?" I asked, not quite believing that all that mattered to her was what other people thought. "Do you really and truly care what they think?"

Annie looked at me. Her face was solemn. "Maybe I care too much about what others think. Not enough about what I think and what the people I love think."

"I think you think too much," I said.

"I think you're right." Annie cuffed me lightly on the good arm. Then she asked, "Petey, do you like me anymore?"

"That's a dumb question. You're my sister. Of course I like you."

"It's just that we haven't been close like we used to be. Before we moved. Before T.C. came."

"We were little kids in San Francisco, before Dad came home. We're not kids anymore. I don't feel a bit like a kid."

"I don't either. I haven't for a long time. Don't you miss San Francisco, Petey?"

"Sure. I miss some of my friends there. Tommy Roberson was the best friend I ever had. I miss him. Some of the others, too, but nobody as much as Tommy."

"I know. I've tried to make new friends here. It

hasn't worked very well. They're nice enough to me, but I don't feel about them the way I did about some of those we left."

"Tanya and Cathy and that bunch? They're B.I.P's, Annie. Born in Pine Hill. You won't ever fit into their crowd, not really. You've seen too much of the world, been too many places to think small, like they do. You know what's out in the world . . . more than they do, anyway. You're bigger than they are, inside. You won't ever feel easy with them."

She reached over and hugged me, very carefully. "Thanks, Petey. Still, I've acted pretty small, sometimes. Like with T.C."

"You sure have . . . but you're still nice people. Dad says it just takes time to get to know each other, sometimes."

"And I don't like living on the farm much, either. Or I didn't. Now I'm not sure. I don't like the way Mom has changed. She never has time for us anymore."

"To play, the way we used to, you mean? Like she does with Brad? We don't need for her to play with us anymore. Not like that. We're not babies, Annie. Brad is. And Mom works all the time, in the house and the garden and driving the tractor when they're hauling hay. You could do that for her."

"I can't drive."

"I can. You can learn. Things are going pretty good now. We can do lots of things together now. Fishing, picnics, that kind of thing."

174

"And riding horses." She looked down at her hands.

"And riding horses. You can still get a riding horse. The Chief wasn't what you needed for that."

"No. But if I hadn't bought him, I might not have either of my little brothers, today," Annie said. "I'm not sorry about the horse I bought. I'll never regret that."

"The sheriff said Mr. Blackburn might give you a horse. A Morgan colt."

"I'm not sure I want another horse, right now, Petey. I'm not sure I need a horse anymore."

"You're a nut," I said. "A real nut."

"You just might be right. A little green nut with the shell all tight up around it. All the doors closed."

"So now what?"

"Open the doors, I guess." She shook her head from side to side. "Or try to."

"What about Tanya and that bunch of snobs?"

"They're not really snobs. Like you said, they haven't been around much. They're covering that up. What do you think of Brenda?"

"She's no glamor girl like Tanya. She's too fat, but she looks at things straight on, and she isn't all the time making fun of people. I don't like people to make fun of other people."

"Neither do I, Petey. And I didn't like them making fun of the Chief, either. Especially not of him."

"What'll they do with him?" I asked. "Bury him, like they did the dead calves?"

175

"I guess so. I suppose Daddy will take care of that."

"Daddy will take care of what?" Mom asked from the doorway.

"You know . . . burying the Chief," Annie said.

"Are you all right, Annie?"

"Sure, just sad."

"Your father talked with T.C. a few minutes ago. He and Evan have made a grave for the Chief under that big pine tree. They haven't closed it up yet. T.C. thought you might like to say good-bye."

Annie slid off the bed. "I sure would."

"So would I," I said, throwing back the covers.

"Not you, Pete. You and the baby are going to stay put for a day or two. Dr. Tucker wants you here so he can keep an eye on you."

"I feel all right," I lied, trying not to wince when I let my legs slide over the edge of the bed. "Anyway, it was me he fought for. I think I've got a right to be there."

Kids don't have many rights in some families, but mine isn't one of those. Dad came in, just then, and nodded in my direction. "If the doctor wants Pete back, I'll bring him back. He does have a right to be there, if he feels like making the trip."

And that settled that.

He went off to get the doctor's O.K. and came back with a pair of pants for me. I don't know where he got them. They were four sizes too big. That was a good thing, though, because they went over the bundlesome bandages on my legs without binding the way jeans would have. I had to wad them up around my waist and pull my belt tight to keep them on. Since Dad picked me up out of the wheelchair and put me into the truck, I didn't do anything like standing around, so there wasn't much danger of losing them. Mom stayed at the hospital with Brad, and just Dad and Annie and I went to say good-bye to the Chief.

21

Nobody talked much. Dad looked straight ahead at the road, paying more attention to his driving than he needed to. Annie fiddled with the edges of her cutoffs, fringing them deeper. I leaned my head against the cool glass of the pickup window and thought about the Chief.

He had been old and unrideable, but there had been a certain grace about him, an air of force that had extended beyond what he was to what he had been. Yesterday, I hadn't seen a sagging old dogmeat horse. I'd seen a wild, free pony from the plains of Montana, a well-trained cutting horse, the wise and beautiful Indian Pony of the sideshow. All that he had been had showed in the way he moved, giving every bit of himself to protecting Brad and me from the dogs.

I don't think he even knew he was a horse. He was just my friend. I know that's crazy, but that's what I was thinking.

T.C. came out to meet us.

"Where's Evan?" Dad asked, nodding toward the jeep.

"He stayed with me today. We called for permission. The principal's office said it would be all right, if you called later, and we made up our work."

Dad smiled at him and looked around.

T.C. smiled back at him. "Evan is out with the Chief. We didn't leave him."

Annie gave him a strange look, but she didn't say anything.

It embarrassed T.C. He seemed to want to explain to her. "When someone, something, fights beside you, dies for you, he deserves more than . . ." He let the sentence drift off lamely, not knowing how to finish it.

Annie put her hand on his arm, very lightly. "I understand. Thank you for making him a place and for waiting for me."

T.C. stumbled over his feet getting out of her way and opening the gate, so we could go over to where Evan sat beside the huge mound of earth.

Dad came around the pickup and took me off the seat as if I didn't weigh almost a hundred pounds and he didn't have a bad leg. He seemed pleased about something. He wasn't nearly as sad as the occasion demanded.

"What are you grinning about?" I whispered.

He wiped the grin from the corners of his mouth, but not from his eyes. "Annie and T.C.," he hissed back at me. "I think she really looked at him for the first time, just now."

Which was a strange thing to say, since T.C. had been living with us for more than a year.

Dad put me down at the edge of the grave, so I could see in. The dreadful sight I'd been expecting wasn't there. The Chief wasn't all stiff and bloated in death. Instead, he looked as if he were asleep, his haunches pulled up under, his front hooves folded under his chest, like a big, contented cat. His head was stretched out in front, eyes closed.

The boys had made a bed of thick, fragrant alfalfa hay to put him on. His mane and tail had been brushed to fine silk and spread out on the straw like the fringe of a Japanese cushion. The drooping underlip didn't show, now. He looked young, as he had yesterday in the fight. Young and sleeping.

"I don't suppose one prays over animals," Dad said softly, his hand on Annie's shoulder. "Just the same, I've been saying prayers of thanks that he was here when we needed him."

"He looks beautiful," Annie said, with a quiver in her voice. "But he was always beautiful to me."

Evan handed Annie the Indian saddle blanket and

the beaded bridle. "We started to put these on him, but we didn't know if you would want us to."

"They're his," she said, touching the rough blanket lightly with the palm of her hand.

Evan slid down the lower side of the hole carefully and shook out the blanket, spreading it over the Chief. It wasn't big enough to cover all of him, but it went over his head and the forepart of his body. Then he laid the beaded bridle beside the blanket and climbed out of the grave.

"Why don't you wait up at the house, Annie?" he asked. "T.C. and I will finish here."

She nodded. There were tears squeezing out around the dark fringes of her eyelashes. Annie never liked for anyone to see her cry. She walked away, not toward the house but to the shed, where the four Angus heifers huddled together, disconsolate.

I pushed myself up. "I'm going with Annie," I said, but I made only two steps before my legs buckled. It was a stupid feeling, not to be able to stand up. Dad put his arms around my shoulders, careful of the bad one.

"Want me to carry you?"

"No. I want to walk, if you'll help me."

"That's what I'm here for," he said without smiling.

Annie didn't look up when we came near, though she must have heard us. She had shaken oats out of the bucket for the heifers. Flakes of oats lay like snow on their curly black foreheads. Annie bent over them, dusting the oats off as they ate, talking softly.

"I'm not going to cry," she said. "I'm not going to cry."

"Why not, sweetie?" Dad asked her. "There's a time for crying."

She buried her face in the furry back of the nearest calf and sobbed as if her heart were breaking. My own throat swelled, and my eyes burned. But I'd already cried my tears for the Chief. I sat back against the fence and let Dad handle this. I never knew what to do when girls cried.

"It isn't fair," Annie sobbed. "It just isn't fair."

Dad looked at me with a sad smile. We'd already had this conversation. He went over to Annie and held her against his chest, rubbing the back of her neck, smoothing the tensions away. "What isn't fair, sweetie?"

"Oh, Daddy. Everything. He didn't have a chance to have a real home. All those years of wandering around. I wanted him to have a home."

Dad was silent for a time, just rubbing Annie's neck gently and patting her on the back. Finally, he held her away from him, so she had to look up at him.

"Annie, nobody ever said life was fair. It isn't. There's nothing fair about it."

Annie wasn't crying so hard, now. She was sniffling some and trying to regain control.

"Honey, Life or Nature or whatever it's called isn't cruel or wicked or kind. It's just relentless. Everything that is born must grow and die. Some sooner, some later. Everything dies. The Chief had a lot of good years. He might have had a few more, but he did

182

something for us in a few days that all the future years could never equal."

"Do you think he knew it'd kill him to fight like that?" Annie asked.

Dad shook his head. "No. Only man knows things like that. Everything else just lives every minute of every day it has. Animals have no way of anticipating death. When the end comes, it comes. No fear. No regret."

"How do you know?" Annie sniffled.

Dad shrugged. "You'll know, too, someday." He let Annie's arms go and came to lean over the fence beside me. He looked very tired.

"Man knows. Sometimes an officer knows when he sends his men out that they'll never make it back. That's when it really hurts. We grieve for the ones who go, but we can't be angry with life, or with whatever god we worship. We have to accept the comings and goings and enjoy what time we have with each other."

"I wanted the Chief to have a home here and time to enjoy it."

Dad's smile was sad, his voice husky. " 'Home is the sailor, home from sea,/And the hunter home from the hill.' He was home, Annie. He knew it when he backed out of the trailer. He wasn't home long, but it was long enough."

The heifers finished the oats and began to jostle around Annie.

"All right now?" Dad asked her.

Annie sniffed once more, then chuckled. "I guess

so. For now. It's hard to cry when you've got a wet nose in your ear." She pushed the calf out of the way and came to stand beside us. "You O.K., Petey? You look like a ghost."

"I feel kinda spooky," I said. "I think I'd better lie down somewhere."

Dad picked me up. "I think you'd better get back to the hospital. I promised I'd bring you right back. You coming, Annie?"

She didn't answer, just looked toward the boys, who were still working with the tractor under the pine tree.

"You can still get another horse for this summer," Dad said, hesitantly, as if he didn't know if this was the time to broach the subject.

"I know, Daddy. But I don't think I need a horse anymore."

I could see the puzzlement on Dad's face. Annie saw it too and smiled at him. "I knew it when I bought the Chief. The Absolutely Perfect Horse is a dream. Something to fill in the empty places. A horse was something to get me into the group I wanted to be with at school. But I have other friends who don't have horses. Brenda doesn't. Evan doesn't."

"But you've wanted a horse forever, Annie," I said.

"I always wanted a horse who would do something wonderful for me. Make me popular, give me all kinds of excitement. Well, the horse I had gave me everything I asked for yesterday. It wasn't the way I planned it. But"—she shrugged—"are things ever like you plan them, Daddy?"

184

"Not very often, I'm afraid." Dad said.

"I know. I guess that's why I don't need a horse anymore. Petey said something about Mr. Blackburn giving me a Morgan colt. Even if he doesn't, Dr. Kurt will let me ride Dancer this summer. I would enjoy a ride, now and then."

"Maybe we could borrow two horses," I said.

"Why, Petey! I didn't think you liked horses!" She sounded surprised.

"I didn't," I said. "But I'm just a little kid. I can still change my mind, can't I?"

Dad shifted my weight and said, "You won't get to trade on that 'little kid' routine much longer, brudder. Annie, I have to take this invalid back to the hospital before the doctor comes looking for him. You'll be O.K.?"

The boys, finished with the grave, were walking toward us.

"I'll be just fine," Annie said, moving away toward them. She linked her arm with T.C.'s. "Come on up to the house, brudder. I'll bet you two guys haven't had a decent meal since yesterday."

I felt Dad give a deep sigh. A looked passed between him and T.C. that had more meanings than I could understand. But I understood enough to make me feel good inside.

Dad put me on the seat of the pickup and came around to the driver's side. He was grinning again and humming something off key under his breath.

"Now what are you grinning about?" I asked him.

He ruffled up my hair and pulled me over close

to him on the seat. "The phoenix is rising, brudder," he said. There was a laugh in his voice.

"I don't know what that means." I yawned. "But I'll think about it when I wake up."